MASTERS OF
NARRATIVE
AND
COLLABORATIVE
THERAPIES

MASTERS OF
NARRATIVE
AND
COLLABORATIVE
THERAPIES

THE VOICES OF ANDERSEN, ANDERSON, AND WHITE

EDITED BY TAPIO MALINEN, SCOT J. COOPER, FRANK N. THOMAS

Routledge
Taylor & Francis Group
New York   London

Routledge
Taylor & Francis Group
711 Third Avenue
New York, NY 10017

Routledge
Taylor & Francis Group
27 Church Road
Hove, East Sussex BN3 2FA

© 2012 by Taylor & Francis Group, LLC

Routledge is an imprint of the Taylor & Francis Group, an informa business

International Standard Book Number: 978-0-7890-3824-1 (Hardback) 978-0-7890-3825-8 (Paperback)

Library of Congress Cataloging-in-Publication Data

Masters of narrative and collaborative therapies : the voices of Andersen, Anderson, and White / edited by Tapio Malinen, Scot J. Cooper, Frank N. Thomas.
    p. cm.
Includes bibliographical references and index.
ISBN 978-0-7890-3825-8 (pbk.)
    1. Narrative therapy. 2. Psychotherapy. 3. Mental health counseling. I. Malinen, Tapio. II. Cooper, Scot J. III. Thomas, Frank N.

RC489.S74M37 2011
616.89'16--dc22   2011005375

Contents

Preface

While editing this book, two of its protagonists, Tom Andersen and Michael White, died. Tom died in May 2007 from injuries incurred when he fell on the rocky Norwegian coast while walking his dog Chico. Michael died in April 2008 from a heart attack he suffered at a restaurant in the evening after a workshop in San Diego.

Together with Harlene Anderson, these premiere therapists have shaped the landscapes of therapeutic practice that have come to be known as dialogical, collaborative, and narrative therapies. Although they have their own diverse approaches, they share a common genuine curiosity for meaning making as a relational process. Whereas the purpose of modernist theory and practice is to solve problems, cure illness, and achieve scientific advancement, one purpose of the work of these three contributors is to explore what sort of social life becomes possible when one way of talking and acting is employed versus another. Within a format that not only allowed them to share their journeys and practices but also to reflect on each other's offerings, what emerges is a glimpse into their wisdom, compassion, and skill that has invited professionals worldwide to seek their teaching.

Within their work, many taken-for-granted ideas and practices are challenged by a more relational framework. For example, the dominant notions of "self" and "individuality" as key elements of emotional health are replaced with connection as one important feature of psychological well-being.

Our skill at seeing processes, or the unity of process and product, has not developed because we are socialized in the Western culture to see only products (things, behaviors, objects, results). For example, we tend to see, experience, and respond to this introduction as a product and not as a moment in an ongoing process (or many processes) that includes the human history of writing, literacy, education, research, history of each specific reader of these words, and so on. We tend also to see, experience, and respond to people as products (identities, labels) rather than as ongoing processes. Yet, each one of us is, at every moment, both being and becoming. Each one of us is constantly under one basic characteristic of our existence, impermanence.

Our wish is that this book could be an example of the process orientation in the work of these premier therapists, and how we in the field together with Harlene—and you as a reader of this book—have all the time and the precious opportunity to be part of the life in the death of Michael and Tom.

Contributors

Tom Andersen

Harlene Anderson tells us how once in an interview Tom was asked: "How would you like people to see you and talk about you?" Tom answered:

> Please pay attention to the words and the work, do not pay attention to me as a person. Please be careful and do not say "Tom Andersen developed the reflecting teams"; it was not me. I was fortunate enough to find good friends and colleagues with whom I could converse and they became part of a flow of ideas and the context. I'd rather be seen as an "invisible" and "unheard" person. I am always looking for a larger context. (Cited in Anderson, 2005, p. 501)

He writes in an article:

> A person takes part in the world as a being. Not the noun Being, but the verb Being: Being-in-the-world, which is: Being-in-(bodily) movements, being-in-language, being-in-conversations, being-in-relationships (being-with-others), being-in-culture, being-in-time (being-in-history), being-in-nature, etc. The change is to be differently in either: movements or language or conversations or relationships. (Andersen, 1997, p. 126)

He writes further: "I have to wait and see how the other responds to what I say or do before I say or do the next thing. The next thing I say or do must be influenced by the other's response to what I just said. The actions are not shaped by any theories or hypotheses, but by a dialogical process." He describes how each of the voices in therapy is given a "home" and how they coexist side by side dialogically "as in every peace work" (Andersen, 1997, p. 130).

In the work of Andersen, Anderson, and White, one can see a shift from a psychology of entities to a psychology of movement and dialogue. Self, other, and relationship are no longer clearly separated entities but mutually forming processes. Self, other, and relations are always in making or self and other form a relational unity in ongoing construction in relational processes. In these dialogical, collaborative, and narrative approaches, the focus of therapy is on the inter-animating process by which the self and the other are mutually authored in and through conversation. Representations of the "other" are contained and located within our "selves." In this view, there can be no "I" without the "other" and no "other" without the "I," and it is language that makes that so. In a genuine dialogue, the quality of the relational space is the key to emergences and openings. It is interesting to notice how this resembles Thich Nhat Hanh's articulation of *interbeing*, a word that describes the interdependence and interconnectedness of all existence, the fact that "everything is in everything else" (Nhat Hanh, 1987).

In the interview Tom did with Per Jensen, just before he died in May 2007, he calls the turning points in his career "crossroads," because he was uncertain to what extent it was his own choice or just to give something up. "The shifts of life around me come by themselves, not by me. The only thing I can do is to take part in them" (Andersen, 2007a, p. 171). Tom lived within a time and space of now that manifested a readiness to respond—after a pause, after a moment of inner dialogue—in a fitting manner to whatever might happen. We can find the first step toward this kind of living, of living "in a moment," as arising out of a special attitude, a felt need to be in a certain kind of selflessly sensitive relationship with surroundings, with both the others and the otherness in them, and be able to answer to the calls that come to us in within those relationships (Shotter, 2007).

Tom's way to be in the relational space was a way to avoid locking into preconceived and fixed ideas that can close off the new possibilities arising in the therapeutic encounter. The mutuality of presence that constitutes relational mindfulness transcends intersubjectivity and moves into realm of interbeing, where seeing and being complete a circuit of reciprocity, a reciprocity of presence. Mishka Lysack describes this kind of dialogue as an exterior form of mindfulness, a special kind of awareness that is a basic element in the ancient wisdom traditions (Lysack, 2008).

The way Tom sees himself is as empty of Tom or as having no self in an egoistic way. This kind of way to be isn't full of his own thoughts, full of activities of his own devices. When one lives this way, the "what is out there" and "what is in here" are completely "in touch" with each other. It is when we fill our body-minds with our own deliberate thoughts about this or about that, that we restrict its ability to be responsive to whatever might happen around us.

When the selves are full, there are vast chasms that separate people. When selves are empty, arising in response to immediate experience, we are all intimately connected to that well from which all experience comes: the "singularity" that cosmologists tell us created a universe from nothing. Looking deeply into emptiness reveals that "each can only inter-be with all the others" (Rosenbaum & Dyckman, 1996). The therapist creates himself or herself creating the client, and the client creates himself or herself creating the therapist. When identity is empty, people encountering each other have a direct experience, in which each other realizes his or her self in the other, the other in his or her self, the other in the other, and the self in the self. When therapist and client meet, there is no need to worry about "self" and "other." Once freed from clinging to the illusory fixed identity, self and world arise to meet and actualize each other, and therapy becomes spontaneous activity. In such spontaneous activity, we rediscover the wonderful joy of a natural interconnectedness.

Tom's way to be in a therapeutic relationship evokes the presence of loving kindness within a dialogic space, thereby providing a relational context for the healing. Relational presence is a ground of not causing harm, a sense of clear seeing with respect and compassion for what it is we see. *Therapeutic love* could be the term to describe this kind of ethical stance. It is a relational stance that is the opposite of *therapeutic violence* (Maturana & Poerksen, 2004). Therapeutic violence takes place in therapy when practitioners impose their will or world perspective on the client in any manner. To prevent this, Tom emphasizes the meaning of pauses in the therapeutic practice.

> We are to be aware of three kind of pauses: (a) the one that comes after exhaling before the next inspiration starts, (b) the one that comes after the person has spoken and thinks to herself of what she just said, and (c) the pause that comes when a reflecting talk occurs, when what was said becomes talked of once more and thereby thought of once more, maybe even in a new way. (Andersen, 2007b, p. 92)

When we are able to respond effortlessly, appropriately, compassionately, and selflessly to the needs of the situation from this space of being, it most effectively contributes to the well-being of others and our selves.

Harlene Anderson

Some years ago I (TM) had the opportunity to interview Harlene Anderson. I was curious to ask her what values dialogue expresses in her work and life. She answered:

> Well, dialogue is a word or a concept that I use to identify a particular kind of process in therapy that in my experience is an inherently generative process. It is something that clients and therapists are doing and are engaged in together. A possibility for something new is inherited in that mutual process. It's a way of talking with each other in which there is more possibility that something will emerge from that conversation that neither person could have brought in independently. It's the back and forth, the criss-crossing, and the combining what you are creating together. Moving in the direction of conversation and dialogue originally came out of our readings and understandings of language and hermeneutics. (Malinen, 2004, p. 73)

Harlene offers us a stance for engaging in the therapeutic relationship as well as a way of expanding our understanding of what we mean by the therapeutic relationship. She is not emphasizing a particular technique or method but rather a way of thinking about knowledge, language, and the therapeutic process, an orientation to therapeutic process that privileges what is happening in the conversation. The focus is on dialogue, not on people, situations, or problems. It positions the therapist in an open manner toward any method of therapy. This different way of being in relationship, this kind of talking, which dissolves not only what you talk about but also the way you talk about it, is the essence of the collaborative approach. It aims to create a space and to facilitate a process in which unworkable problematic situations or narratives can be transformed into workable ones with possibilities. And, once this happens, problems begin often to dissolve.

Harlene makes no attempt to act in a particular manner beyond remaining responsive to the moment. An impetus for her work is to find ways of talking that alert people to the possibility of the unknown, of surprises, of the newness. In any given moment, there are multiple resources for action, and each of these resources has the potential to generate wholly different realities, possibilities, and constraints. Learning to move in and out of these possibilities develops a stance that marks collaborative therapy. While working collaboratively, the therapist is relationally engaged by focusing attention on the conversational process of all those involved (rather than on individuals, objects, problems, or specific strategies). During this process we cannot "know" what forms of relational engagement (what specific actions) will contribute to therapeutic change. The main premise is that meaning is not an individual phenomenon. It is not located in the private mind of a person, and it is not unilaterally determined by one person. Meaning is an achievement of people coordinating their activities together, and it is always transformed in relationships.

When therapy is understood as a conversational process, we can never be certain where it will go. Ironically, one of the qualities we are trained to develop—certainty—inhibits often our ability to move beyond conflict and discord toward transforming dialogic possibilities. Certainty also separates participants by establishing levels of expertise (Amundson, Stewart, & Valentine, 1993). We could call this kind of uncertainty generative because it positions therapist and client in a therapeutic relationship that is responsive to the interactive moment. The therapist is not burdened with being "right" but with being present and responsive. Operating from a position of knowing independently predetermines the possibilities and destroys the co-development of new meaning through the stories and narratives generated in therapy. Our attempts to be good professionals actually can prohibit our ability to be relationally responsive (as professionals) in our conversations with clients. In her book *Conversation, Language, and Possibilities* (1997), Harlene writes:

> I do not think myself as a master consultant or therapist who participates from a meta-position, has privileged knowledge, or has better ideas. I see myself as a guest who drops in on an ongoing conversation. I emphasize that I want only to join the conversation, not to interrupt it or change its course. (p. 167)

According to the tradition of the dialogic philosophy, certainty and orthodoxy belong to the sphere of violent and not appreciative thinking. In this tradition, living in the uncertainty is seen as a human factor with ethical value.

The philosophical stance of the collaborative approach takes us beyond the view of narrative therapy as storytelling and story making and the self as a narrator. Because, unless we extend this view, we succumb to the risk and concerns associated with modernist objectivity: who chooses and who directs the story to be told, how it is told, and what emerges from it. The way we participate as professionals in this narrating process, our position in it and our mode of action, marks the distinction between a modern and a postmodern process. Language is never a representation of the world as it is but rather is a creation of the world as we construct it. Our questions always communicate something about us and what we think; they participate in the construction of their own answers. Questioning is seen as forming. Good questions are those that help to enlarge possible worlds and possible ways of being in relationship.

Harlene's colleague, John Shotter, wants to "reconstruct psychology as a moral science of action (and agency) rather than a natural science of behaviour," and he captures the indeterminacy of meaning whenever someone asks him what he means. He responds, "I don't know. We haven't finished talking yet!" (quoted in McNamee, 2004, p. 15). In the "spontaneous living responsivity" of collaborative practice, the therapist and client construct a discursive domain where the interaction departs from the cultural expectations of therapeutic conversations (e.g., therapist as diagnostic expert). Here, the therapist and client work together to create a conversational space where the therapist's role as expert is not central. "I do not believe that I can teach a person to be a therapist—can you learn someone how to be?—but I can create a space and foster a generative conversational process in which he or she can learn to be," says Harlene (Anderson, 2007a, p. 47). Knowledge is simply a way of being. Because we cannot imagine a human being that would exist without knowing anything, we can say that knowing means simply being. Thus the increasing of knowledge means the increasing of being. One cannot transfer knowledge because no one can transfer being to an other person.

A philosophical stance in a collaborative approach positions us to view therapeutic process as a conversation or dialogue. This stance is very liberating because when we become curious, as opposed to judgmental, about how people engage with each other, we open ourselves to the consideration of alternatives. Doing therapy is also a continuing self-education experience in which the practice of therapy itself is a source of renewal for a therapist as well (Malinen & Thomas, 2009). This source is a critical distinction between those professionals who get bored or burned out by their work and those who do not. The traditional idea of learning is based on the assumption that an independent reality exists, a reality about which we can obtain objective knowledge with the help of scientific methods. The traditional mission of language is to represent, to describe this reality with as much accuracy as possible, and to transfer that knowledge from one person to another. In other words, knowledge is something independent that exists outside of us, a sort of "thing" that we can move into the storage memory of a person. In this dualistic mind-set, another person is an object outside of us who we can explore objectively. An example of this is the diagnostic culture, which often reifies a human being into an object without consciousness. The therapist is an "expert" who has the heavy responsibility for seeing that the therapy process proceeds in the "correct" way. For the well-being of the therapist, it makes a great deal of difference how we have tuned in to perceive and experience this moment we call therapy. In the dualist world where subject and object are separated, we might only experience therapy from the mode of doing: doing diagnoses, doing hypotheses, doing evaluations, doing questions, doing long days while doing therapy, and so on. Our self-appreciation is linked only to our achievements. We are inadequate the way we are and detached from the natural perfection of being. In a nondualistic world where self–other dualism is collapsed, we can experience our work also from the mode of being: We are our words, we are our gestures, we are the consciousness that watches the world with the help of our gaze at the moment. We are resting in our practice and also making a difference. This is what Harlene Anderson mostly does in her work.

Michael White

I (SC) am endeavoring to introduce Michael White, one of the three main contributors to this book, a friend, and colleague, who passed away suddenly from a heart attack during the editing process. It is with enduring sadness and profound respect that I begin this short introduction to Michael's legacy and love for what he did. Because of the vast resource of ideas Michael has left with us, I can't possibly speak to all relevant domains of his contribution to therapeutic conversations and community practice. My intent is to share with you a broad overview that leads toward and provides a foundation for the contribution he has made to this book.

Michael White, from Adelaide, South Australia, along with his cherished friend and colleague David Epston in Auckland, New Zealand, began a relationship of influence, intellectual exchange, and profound exploration that moved away from the traditions of family therapy to spawn narrative therapy. Many credit their collaboration for the resource of diverse ideas that have contributed to narrative practice. Together they describe the atmosphere that typified their unique contribution to therapeutic practice.

> One of the aspects associated with this work that is of central importance to us is the spirit of adventure. We aim to preserve this spirit, and know that if we accomplish this our work will continue to evolve in ways that are enriching to our lives, and to the lives of those persons who seek our help. (White & Epston, 1992, p. 9).

Michael seemed to live and breathe this spirit of adventure in life and practice. He loved to swim, bike, and fly. He loved working with people and exuded warmth and fascination with the details of people's acts of living. He especially loved working with children.

He read widely and far outside traditions of psychology. He drew from a wide range of postmodernist philosophical ideas. The ideas he collected were fused into his theory of practice and were used to describe what he was doing in therapeutic conversations. Michael was drawn to many different realms of thought from anthropology, to ethnography, to philosophy. These influences are evidenced in the coauthored book, *Narrative Means to Therapeutic Ends* (White & Epston, 1990), a book through which many were first introduced to narrative practice. In this first book, much of the foundation of thought informing narrative practice is articulated. Michael and coauthor David Epston write how they draw from the text analogy, noting "that persons give meaning to their lives and relationships by storying their experience and that, in interacting with others in the performance of these stories, they are active in the shaping of their lives and relationships" (p. 13). This premise of narrative therapy that people are interpretive beings constantly trying to make sense of life's events by situating them into stories about their lives and themselves remains key to narrative practice.

All people have stories about their lives and who they are in the world. No single story, however, can represent the totality of life and identity as our lives are multistoried with many possible stories about the same events. There are many events that live outside the problem-saturated dominant stories but have been overshadowed, taken for granted, or not noticed as significant. Michael, with his interest in detail and the events of people's lives that were outside the more dominant problematized accounts, developed a curiosity for the multiple stories of people's lives.

He listened for unique outcomes and initiatives that people had taken that fit more closely with their preferences for their lives. Through inquiry, these events could be further languaged into existence and brought into alternate story lines. This process is referred to as "re-storying." It's a collaborative practice as the person consulting the therapist remains the primary author while the therapist asks questions that help the person move from the known and familiar accounts of his or her life toward what is possible to know and do and toward what fits more closely with that person's preferences for life.

Michael had a passion for questioning the "taken for granted" and great ethical concern for how to participate in therapeutic conversations. Influenced by French philosopher Michel Foucault (1979, 1980, 1984), Michael crafted a narrative approach sensitive to how power and normative expectations operate in people's lives, shape their lives, and can constrain possibility. He developed practices such as externalizing conversations (White & Epston, 1990), which locate problems outside of people as opposed to inside or as representing their identity. This is a very different way of thinking and talking about problems that serves to deconstruct marginalizing, oppressive, normalizing truths. It's a way of talking about problems that while serious, is engaging, at times fun, and freeing from problematized identity claims.

With this practice of externalizing internalized discourse, Michael also brought into view the "small p" political aspects of the work. Externalizing is, in many ways, a countercultural practice and as such is political in assisting people to free themselves from the effects of modern power, normalizing judgments, and the pathologizing of life and expressions of life. Whether the talking metaphor was about out sneaking the sneaky poo (White, 1989), the naughty little phobia (White & Morgan, 2006), fear busting and monster taming (White, 1985), or putting AHD in its proper place (White, 2007), Michael engaged in a practice that made it possible for people to redefine their relationship with the problem and revise their identity in a way that opened possibilities and proposals for action.

Michael was not only a great therapist, he was also an exceptional teacher of his practice. He made often-complex theory and meticulous practice accessible to others through live demonstration; clear, didactic, and compelling stories; and humor. Michael seemed to find geographic metaphors useful to describe his work. In articulating what he was doing in his conversations, he began to utilize the "map" metaphor. Throughout his career he developed several conversation maps that would assist the conversational journey. These are succinctly brought together in his last book *Maps of Narrative Practice* (2007). Michael contends that these maps are not strict steps or rigid guides to be followed in conversations but rather aids to assist one from getting lost in content and to assist the collaboration to move to other territories of thought and action.

Michael's more recent work drew from the Russian developmental psychologist Lev Vygotsky's (1986) "scaffolding conversations" metaphor, the zone of proximal development metaphor, and ideas about concept development. These metaphors seemed to provide Michael with a way to concretely articulate his practices, the social and relational aspect of those practices, as well as the intimate link to the development of personal agency in narrative practice (White, 2007; White & Morgan, 2006). It is in the exploration and adaptation of Vygotsky's ideas that Michael's chapter in this book is situated, archiving his careful and thorough efforts to describe his evolving practice and style.

Jaakko Seikkula

Jaakko is Professor of Psychotherapy in the Department of Psychology at the University of Jyväskylä, Finland. He is mainly involved in developing family and social network–based practices in psychiatry and especially the comprehensive open dialogue approach.

Tapio Malinen

Tapio is a psychologist working in private practice in Finland. He is a teacher in psychotherapy in Helsinki Brief Therapy and Helsinki Psychotherapy Institute, where he teaches solution-focused, narrative, and mindfulness-based practices.

Frank N. Thomas

Frank is Professor of Counseling in the College of Education at Texas Christian University in Fort Worth, Texas, where he teaches brief and family therapy, both of which are competency based. He is also in private practice, providing training, supervision, and psychotherapy to individuals, couples, and families.

Scot J. Cooper

Scot is a practicing therapist and supervisor at H-N REACH, a children's mental health agency in Ontario, Canada, where he provides supervision and walk-in counseling in a large rural community. Scot is also a faculty member at Brief Therapy Training Centres International™, the Gail Appel Institute in Toronto, Ontario, where he teaches brief narrative therapy and competency-based approaches to protection services and inpatient care contexts. Scot is involved in narrative community practice as a community team member of the Neighbouring Communities Project (2007) and the subsequent Pen Pal Initiatives 2008–2010.

John Gurnaes

John is a psychologist doing therapy, supervision, and teaching in private practice in Viby, Denmark.

Yishai Shalif

Yishai is a school psychologist and narrative therapist based in Jerusalem, Israel. He is a director of School Psychological Services in the city of Modiin Ilit. Together with Rachel Paran, he is also the founder and director of the Qesem Center for training, teaching, supervising, and consulting individuals, couples, families, and organizations based on narrative therapy, appreciative inquiry, and Care-Full Conversation™ for multicultural dialogue.

Introduction

The unique gathering of Tom, Harlene, and Michael took place in Hämeenlinna, Finland, at the Common Ground–Versatile Practices Conference, where they came together to present their ideas and practices in June 2004.

Contributing to the richness of their stories are the reflections of Professor Jaakko Seikkula and an international group of colleagues. Jaakko is known internationally as one of the developers of a highly successful approach for working with psychosis known as open dialogue treatment. The members of the international reflecting group are John Gurnaes, a family therapist from Dispuk, Denmark, and Yishai Shalif, a senior school psychologist and narrative therapist from Jerusalem, Israel. With curiosity and interest, the outsider discussants invite the principal contributors into dialogue, serving to draw out ideas about Wittgenstein, dialogue, philosophical stance, and the scaffolding metaphor, among other ideas. These reflections are like invitations to continue to refine the ideas and to continue to strive for knowledge.

As a fitting beginning, Tom Andersen invites us along to navigate the "forks in the road" he faced in his emerging career. However, as you read, the significance of these "forks" becomes clear by their immense influence on the field. In particular, Tom outlines the shift from either/or thinking to both/and thinking while sharing how physical therapists Aadel Bülof-Hansen and Gudrun Øvreberg touched his thinking and practice. These women made personal contributions to his thinking by serving as the catalysts for the early part of his journey. Tom further gives us a glimpse into the emergence of the reflecting team concept. This is an idea and practice that began to level the hierarchy between therapist and client and that later contributed to Michael White's pursuit of outsider witnessing practices. It's an example of the generative influence of striking yet risky ideas for their time.

Through a touching transcript of a session with a mother and 19-year-old daughter, Tom almost slows time as he introduces us to his practices in action. With micro-attention to language and curiosity that allows him to take his time, the reader is introduced to how "words are like universes travelling by." For Tom, words have many meanings in them, even big stories and landscapes, which he dawdles in while seeking rich meaningful connections with others. He listens to every word to see how the words affect the other person. Tom's practices of language are a central part of his life work.

Harlene's voice then takes center stage as she paints the picture of her experiences in collaboration with women in Bosnia. However, those experiences are first firmly planted on a rich philosophical foundation that permeates her practices. For Harlene, the idea that conversation needs to be dialogic is heartfelt. She notes they are a shared inquiry about the issues at hand—jointly examining, questioning, thinking, and reflecting. You will sense the importance of trust and respect in her words and practices. As she outlines the aspects of her philosophical stance, ideas about the mutually transformative aspects of conversations, the not-knowing curiosity, and conversational partners begin to shape what will capture you in her story of her time in Bosnia. Today these concepts continue to add a great deal to the field and to the lives of those who consult therapists.

Entering Bosnia begins a touching recount of Harlene and her colleague Patricia Blakeney's ability to be present to the needs and wants of women working in a nongovernmental organization. In the face of hopelessness and through genuine openness and connection, they begin to center the voice and local knowledge of these women, honoring their pain and discouragement while, ever so gently, punctuating the beginnings of a plan for the future. It is a touching example of her philosophy in action.

Fittingly, Michael White, cofounder of the narrative therapy tradition contributes a chapter that is a clear example of the frontiers of collaborative postmodern therapies. Through the introduction of the theory and application of Vygotskian ideas, Michael excites the reader about what is possible to know and do in a therapeutic conversation. He outlines the zone of proximal development and introduces the concept of scaffolding to assist people to traverse the distance from the known and familiar to what is possible to know. These ideas and practices translate into concrete ways to sustain people's initiatives in their lives, to bring them into prominence as a counter to problem stories and limiting identity conclusions.

Michael masterfully demonstrates scaffolding distance conversations through the micro-analysis of a session with a young boy and his mother. He will take you through the incremental crafting of his questioning, which contributes to a significant distancing from the known ideas of a boy who was "generally considered incapable of reflecting on his life, unable to foresee the consequences of his actions, and relatively incapable of taking responsibility for his own life." Where they finish not only will instill hope but is a significant step into a different knowing that opens options for living and brings forward the wisdom and life skills the family has always utilized.

Throughout this book, you will be inspired and touched not only by the main examples but also through the small detours each presenters adds. These are detours and stopoffs to reflect on each other's practices, or to tell a short story of a meaningful time in their own professional and personal journeys.

1

AN OPENING TRIALOGUE

Scot: Conversation is at the heart of therapeutic practice and this book, so I thought it fitting to invite you both to begin a conversation about what's to come for the reader, your understandings of the common ground that connects our three contributors, and the versatile practices that have sprouted from their contribution to the field. Tapio, perhaps you could set the stage for us saying a bit about how the exchange among the three principals in this book—Tom Andersen, Harlene Anderson, and Michael White—came to happen and add your reflections on those few days?

Tapio: The history has its history. Before coming together to the seminar this book is documenting, Harlene, Michael, and Tom had all had their separate, individual workshops in Finland. As a matter of fact, it might be that the seed for the meeting that this book archives was laid down already in the late 1980s. Jaakko Seikkula, Professor of Psychotherapy at the University of Jyväskylä, invited Harlene Anderson and Harry Goolishian from the Houston Galveston Institute (HGI) to the Hospital of Keropudas in northern Finland a couple of times, where these three open-minded and creative professionals explored and further developed a way of practice called the open dialogue in Finland and collaborative practice in the United States. Also, Tom had had long-time contact with these three people around the issue of how to do therapy with dignity and within a collaborative space. So I guess, in many ways, this extraordinary gathering in June 2004 reflected the definition of the Grand Man or the Woman quite well, which I very much like: The Grand

Man or the Woman is one who sees further than the others because he or she stands on the shoulders of the others.

For me those few days together with these skillful practitioners of deconstruction through languaging in psychotherapy were the death of the Believer and the birth of the Seer. And what does this mean? Well, a certain therapy approach and its theory—whatever it might be—can make one a Believer, justify one's beliefs and conception of the world, and give a home to a lonely and separated therapist ego. Doing so gives protection and safety and a possibility to identify with something larger in order to create meaning in our lives as therapists. But the experiences that give birth to the Seer are also the ones that push you to emptiness, breaking, destroying, and transforming one's world of meaning in a thorough way. After that, the world is not the same place anymore: You can see differently.

One common ground for these three practitioners is that they have the skillful means to make transformations possible. They do this by creating conversations with the people they are working with, creative interpersonal exchanges that open up new territories of life and practices of living. In these dialogues, both clients and therapists can find new possibilities in the landscape of the mind that previously was seen and experienced as solid, fixed, unchanging, and limiting. By continuously deconstructing and reconstructing our inner realities, they collaboratively co-create mental space that destroys our former ways of experiencing the world and ourselves.

According to the central ethos of postmodernism, Michael, Tom, and Harlene don't want to obscure people's minds with universal and complex theories, or as Tom expresses it, "to use frozen words to describe something very dynamic and always moving." Instead of theories, Harlene is talking about a philosophical stance, Michael said that he was just talking about ideas, and Tom expressed that theory for him meant "to look." For example, we can feel what loneliness means to another human being in our bodies.

We don't have to make facts correspond to the theory, we don't have to explain anything; we can just let our preferred descriptions organize our brain in the way that produces fruitful action.

So one thing that is common for these three "collaborationists" is that they have no unified theories of human behavior, personality, normative individual development, health and disease, or the causes of psychological problems. Instead, their theories can be considered a philosophical stance on the nature of knowledge, the social construction of reality, and the creative potential of language (Mahrer, 1987). Instead of being a scientific theory on human behavior or personality, this stance offers us clues regarding how to construct change-inspiring conversations.

Of course there are also clear differences in their versatile practices, but before going into them I am quite curious to hear whether my words and the meanings they carry have touched you in any way. And if so, in what way?

Scot: Tapio, thanks for starting us off. I wanted to pick up on your piece about the philosophical stances of these "collaborationists," as you call them. What emerges across philosophies of these three practitioners, to me, is a relational ethics of practice. This ethics-based practice involves paying great attention to the possible effects therapeutic conversations have on people's real lives. This ethics of practice calls for great responsibility in crafting how the conversations are shaped and shared and how the concepts of both life and identity are talked about. It's an ethic that at times juxtaposes the grand narratives circulating within our cultures with the more marginalized narratives about how to be in the world.

I remember Michael responding to a workshop audience member's question (actually, it was more of a statement) that our practices need to be evidence based. He replied politely, "Well, I imagine you could make anything work if you exerted enough power and influence." To me, this was a call to not only look at the outcomes to which our practices contribute but also pay great attention to how we go about contributing to outcomes. Is there not a different ethic in co-creating conversation, in assisting people to name their experiences, and in practicing in ways that assist people to come to know themselves through their preferred views? I would suggest there is, and it's how Michael, Tom, and Harlene put that ethic into practice that stands out for me.

I think this ethic of practice was evidenced in Tom's pioneering of the reflecting team as a means of bringing greater transparency to therapeutic conversations. Michael extended the ethic into the realm of identity in structuring outsider witnessing practices where a series of re-tellings are structured and shared with the participant (White, 1985). Harlene takes up the ethic in the pursuit of collaboration and with an eye on maintaining open dialogue.

Frank: I too have been moved by the work of all three pioneers, at different times and in different ways. To start, I got to know Harry Goolishian, Harlene's mentor and later collaborator, in the early 1980s. His untimely death in 1991 only spurred me to further study thought regarding deconstruction. Harry was constantly changing throughout his career. A voracious reader, Harry had difficulty putting books down. I once had to drag him out of the University of Texas bookstore so we would not be late for an important meeting we had arranged, and he was reluctant to end his perusal and purchasing. Harry's approaches and therapy were a compilation, embodying a history of psychotherapy. Strategic, Mental Research Institute (MRI), and brief traditions influenced his way of seeing, thinking, and acting. In the late 1980s, Harry and Harlene, his close colleague at the Galveston Family Institute (later renamed the Houston Galveston Institute, or HGI), floated the concept of "not-knowing" on the sea called family therapy. In my own work, I have made various attempts to implement the not-knowing stance for over 20 years, and it has both reinforced my own second-order cybernetic view of the world and transformed my psychotherapy practice. Long before

Insoo Kim Berg and others blended not-knowing into their solution-focused therapy (SFT) assumptions, I saw the value of this stance and worked to privilege the client's view and experience more than my own. Although this is a daily work-in-process, I know the Goolishian-Anderson stance of not-knowing has changed the course of my work more than any other concept over the past 20 years.

In like fashion, Tom Andersen's cautious approach to knowing and respectful ways of introducing difference have led me to new forms of curiosity. Tom's massage metaphors from his early work created sensitivity in my conversations as I sought to find a "just right" balance between too-different and too-similar. I found a sense of wholeness-in-therapy from his reflecting team and inner-outer dialogue contributions that was largely unconscious until recently. That is, I have found that my work is much more centered on being than doing (see Malinen & Thomas, 2009) as I attend to more than just the verbalization being exchanged in the room. My gut, my heart, my focus, my thoughts, and my expression through words, signals, and nonverbal communication all move me to be present in a therapeutic way. In my personal times with Tom, he was a conundrum, gentle and direct, philosophical and bluntly honest, a wonderful dinner partner who never seemed to lack patience as a listener. As the reader can see from the exchanges within this book, Tom was not afraid to confront as well as carefully question. What he liked, he loved; what he disliked, he challenged; and what he felt was dishonest, he confronted.

Finally, the narrative practices of Michael White and his colleague David Epston burst upon the scene in the late 1980s when I was learning other postmodern/poststructural models, and their social philosophy and ethic of responsibility stood in contrast to some models (such as SFT) and in agreement with others (including feminist approaches). Separated by 9,000 miles and unfamiliar with his work, I discovered that Michael and I were both evolving from a first-order cybernetic model we had embraced in the 1980s (we both had chapters in the same book on eating disorders—see Harkaway, 1987; Keeney et al., 1987; White, 1987), and I found his transformation intriguing. Drawing from philosophers largely unknown to family therapy, Michael brought a social conscience to the forefront of our discipline. He was also unafraid to experiment—anyone who knows his oeuvre has witnessed his evolution from metaphors of text to social witness to Vygotsky (as seen in this book). And he was unapologetic to those who would not change with him or tried to restrict him to his past ideas. Finally, Michael was a rock star in family therapy, but he always chose to take risks that had the potential to blemish his status. With the exception of the late Insoo Kim Berg, I believe I have seen more videotapes of Michael White doing therapy demonstrations than any other pioneer of the past 20 years, a testament to his desire to both press forward theoretically and assist those in need.

Scot, I love your quotation from Michael about evidence-based practices and power. It exemplifies the best of all three of the scholar-practitioners we are honoring in this volume—Michael, Harlene, and Tom. None of these collaborationists force, pry, or take charge; all seek common ground for experience, understanding, and change. To paraphrase my friend Lynn Hoffman, our field has been transformed by the work of these innovators who have created interconnecting roots that support us all.

Tapio: As I read your words and the meanings my culturally and socially conditioned mind constructed out of them, something happens: I become aware of my "intentional ears." Some words are very alive for me; they touch me deeply, move my thinking, and connect me to something that is very precious in my life. I want to connect myself to these words. Some words are more neutral. How is this? I think our "collaborationists" have also answered this question on our behalf.

In order to function ethically in our work, we have to be aware of those factors that underline our actions. How can we contribute helpfully to people's quality of life without "colonizing" them with foreign ideas and practices that obscure or eradicate their local knowledge? Mindful attention to how we choose to view the persons we work with is all about power. To experience the therapeutic relationship as the outgrowth of ethical commitment where real, good, and beautiful are "con-joint-ly" constructed through the common process of meaning making is in contrast to a notion of relationship as a strategic tool to "effect change" (Paré, 2010, p. 5). For the psychotherapist, this means an invitation to relational responsibility where power is used as an opportunity to join people in reclaiming the richness of their lives. Far from objectivity and neutrality, this calls us to ethical caring, a profoundly passionate commitment to others.

In order to be part of this ethics-based practice, we have to be ready and open to explore, to unpack not just how our actions within the power relations of therapy affect other human beings but also how they affect us. The goal of this kind of exploration is not to teach our clients what is meant by the concept of a "good life" but to co-create an open space where we can together search how to live a "good life." In this intersubjective space, ethics is based on the process of practicing the mind to answer the existential, fundamental questions in an experience-based manner, questions like, What is the meaning of *practicing* as the modifier of the quality of experience and deepened understanding? What is the nature of "the self"? What is the place of compassion when with our fellow human beings?

Frank, for me one of the interconnecting roots of these innovators is the openness to explore what ethically wholesome and skillful actions mean for the therapist. To be willing and to have the courage to deconstruct our own normalizing judgments, which exert control over ourselves and our clients, is a good example of this ethical practice. Finally, Tom has also pointed toward what stillness means for us as a political action. At this moment we need less greed, anger, and ignorance instead of more 5-year plans or expansive profit thinking.

I think that when our work—as you experience yours to be—is more centered on being than doing, the collaborative dialogues can also be understood as exterior and transformative forms of mindfulness. According to Mishka Lysack (2008), they are considered as forms of co-meditative practices where intersubjectivity may deepen through mindful listening to the forms of "inter-being" and the compassionate witnessing of suffering of others. During this kind of conversation, there is usually a shift from psychology on entities to a psychology of movement and dialogue where self, other, and relationships are mutually forming processes.

We may know all the rules about loving your neighbor as yourself, but as long as we don't "see" it, it is just a concept. Scot, for me the ethics-based practice is about being it, not just knowing it. I think this is also manifested in different ways in the work of our collaborationists. This kind of relational ethic offers the therapist a deeply privileged position: We can be transported through our work to the new territories of life and practices of living. And for this we can thank the people who come to these common conversations with us.

Scot: I want to touch first on Frank's thoughts and then I will offer what Tapio's comments sparked for me. Frank, your historic account of the emergence of the ideas and practices common to Harlene, Tom, and Michael had me thinking about the context in which they were developing. As a Canadian, I am aware of the current pressures and demands in the field to demonstrate evidence-based practices. This has been understood at times to mean adherence to specific models of therapeutic practice. A common criticism has been that such strict adherence won't allow for innovation. I imagine our collaborationists were not doing things according to the dominant discourses of their time. Yet all three crafted practices have moved the field to new places. At the "Catching the Winds of Change 3" conference, David Epston, who co-founded narrative therapy with Michael, highlighted how historically many therapeutic conversations sponsored practices that sought confession or culpability, which could be experienced as degrading of people. He went on to speak about his efforts to meet people through their "wonderful-nesses" and to create space for the insider knowledges to be recognized and used. These conversations, to me, are a very different journey in themselves than many of the more dominant schools of therapy being taught. So Frank, I wonder if you could say some more about what the forces in the field Harlene, Tom, and Michael were able to resist and move away from?

Frank: Well Scot, my historical view is biased, of course, but I do situate the rise in prominence for all three in a time of raging change here in the United States. Only one of our collaborationists is from the United States, but much of the psychotherapy field—research, academic publication, training, book sales, and so on—is driven by what mental health professionals in this country embrace. From the early 1950s through the mid-1980s, the systems-cybernetic view dominated both theory and model development. Historical figures like Gregory Bateson, Jay Haley, Cloé Madanes, John Weakland, and Salvador Minuchin made their marks, and their somewhat mechanistic views of human interaction guided the thinking and actions of most family therapists. The rising challenge brought by poststructural and postmodern thinking, led by honest confrontations from feminist scholars and clinicians, created space for new approaches. These new approaches were not limited by the field or metaphors of family therapy; their influence began in many areas (psychiatry, social psychology, business, organizational psychology, and psychotherapy in general) and gained momentum rapidly. The field of psychotherapy was hungry for new approaches that promoted ethical practices focused on the human experience. Some gained worldwide notoriety; SFT founders Insoo Kim Berg and Steve de Shazer were quite influential during this time, and the SFT approach is now pervasive, even commonplace, in

international psychotherapy practices. Others with different emphases, like Bill O'Hanlon, Michele Weiner-Davis,
Lynn Hoffman, and Karl Tomm, also became influential
postmodern voices in North America. Evidence-based therapies founded on modernist principles compete with postmodern approaches in the academy and marketplace, but all
models have found followings and show future promise.

Regarding our book's three principals, Michael and Tom
were quite well known prior to this upheaval in Australia and
Norway, respectively, and the uncertain times of the 1980s
and 1990s in the U.S. psychotherapy arena allowed them to
find a global voice. Harlene's work made a significant shift
during this 20-year time period as well. I still remember
Harlene and Harry Goolishian conducting a workshop at
my Texas institute in 1989, during which they spelled out
the acronym B-R-I-E-F-T-H-E-R-A-P-Y with the first let-
ters of each major point in their clinical approach . . . so, they
made quite a shift in the next few years! The collaborative
language systems (CLS) approach became more prominent
in Texas in the 1990s, expanding into Mexico and drawing
attention from others around the globe. Later shortened to
collaborative therapy, Harlene continues to lead a dedicated
following and conducts training in her approach throughout the world. Tom's reflecting team and Michael's narrative practices developed followings as well. Tom was a close
collaborator with Harlene, making many visits to the Gulf
Coast of Texas to work, train, and learn with those closely
tied to HGI. Michael's influence was much more global,
as narrative practices expanded far beyond Australia and
New Zealand through, for example, the work of Stephen
Madigan from Canada, Jill Freedman and Gene Combs
from Chicago, and many others throughout the world.

Overall, I see the work of Tom, Harlene, and Michael
as separating from, rather than overcoming or compet-
ing with, other practices. After the first few Therapeutic
Conversations conferences in the early 1990s, narrative
therapy practices created its own forum separate from

other therapy traditions like SFT and CLS. Practitioners of narrative approaches formed their own journals, training institutes, and conferences. Meanwhile, collaborative therapists tied to Harlene's ideas developed their thinking and focused their training through HGI, the Taos Institute, and annual summer institutes in Mexico. Only Tom seemed to "float" among various institutions, organizations, and models/approaches, loaning his expertise and contributing his ideas without building a school or model-specific following. I believe all three—Michael, Tom, and Harlene—seemed deeply moved to promote their ideas without force, honoring others' voices while enthusiastically advancing their passions and practices.

Scot: Tapio, we have been referring to our three contributors as *collaborationists*. This is a new word, in a sense. I'm wondering about this word and what it means. I see Michael's practice as collaborative in that he seeks to build upon insider knowledge yet employs a set of skills he has honed over time, such as the ability to scaffold conversations. I'm not sure that Harlene and Tom would see that practice in the same vein of collaboration as their work. So I'm curious about how you see these three collaborating in their conversations and how their practices may be different or divergent? Could you say more about this?

Tapio: Well, as Wittgenstein has pointed out, the meanings of words cannot be found in dictionaries; they are co-created in the contexts in which they are being used. Likewise, the word *collaborationist* was created in the context of this trialogue, and its personal meaning for me was also founded in my meetings with Harlene, Michael, and Tom. It has kind of embodied the live interactions with these three with you both within this trialogue and also in my encounters with my clients. I think that it is also natural or even inevitable that your meanings might be different from mine and our meanings will develop further and change during the meaning-making processes.

People don't generate thoughts, feelings, and actions out of thin air; they do so from cultural locations. Our conversations with our clients happen always in a "mirrored room" surrounded by cultural influences reflecting back upon the words spoken (Paré, 2010, p. 6). At the moment, for me a *collaborationist* means a practitioner who is guided by the ethic, which advocates for the co-invention of the direction in therapy in a very special and careful way. It's a way that keeps the clients' values in the center of the practice without diminishing the rich contributions therapists may bring to the conversation. It's a way that involves tapping into clients' skills and resources, even when these are not particularly visible to them in the midst of their struggles. This is a notion of local or insider knowledge, and a collaborative conversation is an expression of cultural respect—a way of working with, rather that working on, the persons who consult us (Paré, 2010).

Collaborationists usually create conversations with others in such a way that meaning making becomes world making and allows all of the participants to access their creativities and develop possibilities where none seemed to exist before (Anderson, 2001). There is a constant influence between two subjects in dialogue where knowledge of the Other arises between partners in an open field of possibility. This relationship is an ongoing, mutual process of negotiation of meaning sentence by sentence. In this constitutive process, the therapist is creating him- or herself by creating the client, and the client is creating him- or herself by creating the therapist.

In the sea of collaboration, there are many waves that, although having different appearances, are manifestations of the same Ocean, the same One-ness. In the work of our practitioners the process of collaboration appears also in three different ways. David Paré, Brian Richardson, and Margarita Tarragona (2009) have written about intentionality and responsivity in dialogue in a way that has helped me to understand—within one dimension—the diversity of these waves in this Ocean.

When our practice is characterized by intentionality, it is usually informed by active choice-making, which involves selecting from options presented in clients' talk. Narrative therapists usually view persons who consult them as having come under the influence of problem-saturated stories. A narrative collaborationist is joining them with preconceived question sequences, which Michael used to call maps. With these maps the therapist is opening a linguistic space for "re-authoring" clients' lives. This becomes a site for "rich story development," a thickening of particular accounts of identity aligned with a person's hopes and commitments. The intention is to scaffold conversations that build agency, an ability to perform cherished values in the face of life's challenges. One can also say that by deconstructing power–knowledge relations, this kind of collaboration is always a political action with small "p."

A practice oriented to responsivity is primarily informed by the client's contributions, utterance by utterance. These conversations emphasize the importance of being with the client, following the conversation closely, and spontaneously responding to anticipated "striking moments." During this process, a slow shift in meaning occurs without specific interventions or preconceived list of questions. In this collaborative dialogue, problems usually "dissolve"; they do not always go away or get "solved" but in some way they become more workable (Paré, 2010). Healing depends more on a shift of consciousness than an uncovering or resolution of conflict.

Tom Andersen also integrated what might be called "bodied knowing" into this conceptualization of collaborative practice. His was a sensory, highly personal way of working involving a person's whole being, a skill to see or hear how the words of the speaker are also moving him- or herself. This ability of Tom's might have been inherited from his close collaboration with physiotherapists and his special relationship with silence.

I am sure that all of our collaborationists might say (and experience) that they are also integrating intentionality and responsivity in their work as all therapists might be doing to some extent. In spite of this, one can also say that Michael was probably more on the intentional side of this conceptual dimension than Tom, with Harlene being somewhere in between. Saying this, I am also aware that this kind of positioning of our "collaborationists" is always somehow artificial in the poststructuralist Ocean of experience.

Scot: Before we close this conversation, I feel it would be important to note additional areas in which our primary collaborationists are more divergent in practice. One particular area is the use of audience in therapeutic practice. Tom's use of reflecting teams, to me, was a use of audience as a means not only to increase transparency in the process but also to introduce multiple perspectives from which people (clients) could draw.

In his later years, Michael saw finding an audience for the emerging preferred developments in people's lives as an essential part of his practice. He utilized various ways to do this, such as letter writing, using stuffed animals, phone conversations, e-mail, and outsider witnessing. He saw the use of audience as intimately linked to the nonstructuralist ideas that view the "self as constructed in relation to others, as a social and collaborative achievement" (White & Morgan, 2006, p. 108). The use of recruiting audience to preferred developments was a way to thicken the alternative and preferred identities of people. I believe this is where Michael's (and of course, David Epston's) practices have added to the field in significant ways.

Where Tom and Harlene employ reflecting teams, Michael structures sessions as definitional ceremonies using outsider witnessing practices, drawing heavily from the work of cultural anthropologist Barbara Myerhoff (1982, 1986) with elderly Jews in Los Angeles, California. The "re-tellings" of outsider witnesses in therapeutic conversations are specifically structured. Michael used to stress the importance of structuring these re-tellings, noting that leaving them to chance could become hazardous, as habits of cheerleading, complimenting, encouraging, or centering one's own story may occur. Michael chose to structure these tellings (see White, 2007) to invite people to speak in ways that would give them a sense that their lives are linked, resonating in some way with others. Participants often experienced the process as highly acknowledging of their lived experience but also brought into the conversation how the therapist was also touched by the participants' story. In this way, Michael is recognizing how therapeutic conversations give to others. The structure for the process Michael has proposed seems to move in a different direction than both Harlene and Tom. This is not to say that Tom and Harlene don't have some structure to their use of audience but rather to note that in narrative practice, the use of audience takes a much more central place in re-storying.

I continue to be moved and warmed by how re-tellings contribute to how the people with whom I have therapeutic conversations come to know themselves differently and become linked to a broader social circle. I think there is a great deal of unexplored practice in relation to how audience is used in therapeutic practice. However, this unexplored or less explored territory may go against more traditional notions of confidentiality. Again, for me I think about how I can have the kinds of conversations with people that they want to leave and share with others and include others in witnessing and celebrating. However, I do acknowledge Tom and Harlene for their contributions to the exploration of therapeutic conversations and audience.

Tapio: I would like to end the first part of our trialogue with the Wittgenstein quote Tom used in his contribution within this book. "When you are looking for similarities in different kinds of games, for instance chess or football or cricket, just look, don't think" (Wittgenstein, 1968, p. 37). This reminds me that in using language we are unable to "tell the truth" about anything. Because our words are not maps of the world, but born out of communal convention, there is no final or accurate or foundational account of the process of constructing the realities of Harlene, Tom, and Michael. So this trialogue might also be simply a pointer to the rich world of our pioneers, the world that can never be fully described with words. Or the words might just hide everything that is not words, full multidimensional of splendour of their life work.

At this moment people living in modern cultures suffer an extreme degree of separation and alienation that was unknown in earlier times—from society, community, older generations, nature, tradition, their bodies, their feelings, and their humanity itself. While the doing mode of our mind would like to explain "the truth" in the work of our collaborationists, the being mode doesn't have to believe in it—it can just look and "see." The feeling of not-being-separate might also emerge in the heart of accepting what is different.

2

WORDS—UNIVERSES TRAVELING BY

TOM ANDERSEN

Until his death in 2007, Tom Andersen served as Professor of Social Psychiatry at the Institute of Community Medicine, University of Tromsø, Norway. His influential ideas about reflecting teamwork have contributed significantly to addressing relations of power in therapy and have opened new possibilities for respectful conversations. Tom was considered to be one of the most humble and admired therapists in the field.

Forks in the Road

I have decided to tell about what I've done for the last few years, which has been to look back to try to describe the professional walk I have been on. I have decided to use the word *walk*. It has been a very slow walk similar to the speed we have when we collect mushrooms. This has been a walk in reality with stop-offs to walk in the mind. It might sound pretentious to talk about one person's walk, but I do it because I believe strongly that each of us is generated very differently as professionals. We are much more personal than the authorities have led us to believe.

On this walk, looking back, it has been interesting to identify the forks in the road, and there have been at least 30 important forks. One cannot continue to walk on both roads; one has to take one and leave out the other one. It has been interesting to try to clarify what made me go down one road and not the other. If those are to be called "choices," the choices have been very emotional. I'm speaking as an academic. There have been very few rational choices. It has also been interesting to notice that most of the choices have been to leave out something and say, "I cannot continue on that road anymore." I had to get out of it; it felt too uncomfortable to continue. That is interesting—not the choice of the road to follow, but to leave out things.

There were two important forks in the road before I became a professional. One road was called "indifference," and the other was "endure and never be indifferent." It is so easy to become indifferent: "We cannot do anything in Iraq, so let's let it all happen." I think we must not be indifferent to the dividing of people who want to stay together, not be indifferent to obedience or disobedience. There is a lot not to be indifferent to. A Catholic priest in Asunción, Father Miguel, said, "Many times we feel hopeless, impotent in Paraguay and when we feel powerless, we never become indifferent." Good words!

The second fork in the road was to leave the mainstream and go to the margins, to avoid repeating what everybody else did. Out there one can meet other interesting people, also preferring to search in the margins. Jaakko, for instance, Harlene, Michael; there are many people who prefer the margins. So passing those two forks in the road was important.

When I became a professional and I was a medical doctor in the country, I was determined to not be interested in sophisticated, rare conditions, but to seek the most common and the most difficult. The most common were people having pain in their body such as pain in the neck, shoulders, back, or stiffness and tiredness—ordinary complaints. I was attracted to that and to conversations with people; very different conversations with people who had, somehow, fallen out of balance. The body was a focus of interest: the movements of the body and when the movements of the body froze or stopped, or when the body became less lively.

Then I went into psychiatry for different reasons. At that time, when the patients came into the hospital in Tromsø, my hometown, it took a very short time before it was difficult to reconnect them back to where they came from. With that came a rational choice: We must leave the hospital and move out to the communities to protect this connection. We must do something out there, so that people do not need to be disconnected from those they want to be connected with.

There was also an emotional component in the choice to go out. I could see the quiet patients daring not to express so much. They looked like refugees. They had lost their homes, and that felt very uncomfortable. So we had to go out, which we did, and that small choice was a big step. We left the perspective of individuality, which we worked within at the hospital. We had seen people as varied, as individuals, independent of their surroundings. We tried to look into the person to know what was going on. By going out, we adopted a contextual perspective and understood human beings as a part of their surroundings. At that time, we grabbed the idea of family therapy, which said the person belonged to a context, and every context changes with time. So "context" and "time" became important words.

One more thing happened in this seemingly small change, which has turned out to be a very important fork in the road. That was to leave the language of the hospital and turn to ordinary daily language. In the language of pathology, we described people in terms of their failures. When we went out, we were attracted to describing them in their successes in ordinary words. I will come back to the importance of how we described those we were in relation to.

We did family therapy as one did those days; we were very active, and we even used the word *interventions*, which made us think we were at war with the families. Usually we all dealt with two main questions, no matter if we came from Finland, Norway, the United States, or Australia. We were mostly dealing with two big questions when we came to a problematic situation. One question was "What is this?" and the other, "How can I go on, how can I proceed without being in a problem?" Actually, ordinary people are more interested in the latter question than the first one, and that created a new fork in the road. I decided to give priority to the question "How should I go on?" before the question "What is this?" I will come back to that later as it was an important choice in the academic world.

Frozen and Living Ways of Being

After the families asked themselves, "What is this?" or "What shall we do?" they also gave answers to their own questions. We thought that if their answers didn't help them out of the problem, their answers to the questions contributed to the problem. We wanted them to think differently and to do something different. Being interventionists, we said, "Instead of what you have been thinking, think this, and instead of what you have done, we think you should do this." With those short words *instead of,* we slapped them. It feels very uncomfortable to be slapped. It's very uncomfortable to slap someone. The families responded by disagreeing with what we said.

They said, "You don't understand."

"Yes, we understand fully."

"You don't know us too much."

"Yes, we know you well."

That was a very uncomfortable place to be, to constantly be fighting with the families. Then, almost out of the blue, we started to speak to them very differently one day in the fall of 1984. We took out the phrase "instead of" and replaced it with the phrase "in addition to." We said, "In addition to what you thought, we have been thinking this!" "In addition to what you have been doing, could you consider doing this?" The struggle with the families disappeared, and it immediately felt much more comfortable to be in the room. What happened in the moment we changed from "instead of" to "in addition to" was a big ideological and philosophical change. We moved from either/or to both/and thinking. We started to generate new ways of being and thinking of ourselves.

Either/or are very important words in the physical sciences, which investigate the part of reality that we can see. The part of reality that is frozen, where the movements are very, very slow, is like the movements of a stone. A stone is constantly congealing, freezing, coagulating, and it's on the way to be congealing more. Because the movements are so slow, the moment in that part of the world is endless. We had been treating families as if they were frozen. It's a very, very, very dangerous way to be as a therapist. If we treat someone as if they are frozen, they become frozen. So I'm very glad the families protested, because that helped them to stay alive. This "either/or" belongs to the part of reality that is frozen and visible, whereas "both/and" is in the part of reality which is living and visible. I wondered, "How did this happen, this change to the both/and perspective?"

Just See, Hear, Feel, and Not Think

Now let me tell you about a lady who was a physical therapist and who helped me to understand how one should work with the stiffness in the body, when the movements in the body stop and the body and the person become less lively. Her name was Aadel Bülow-Hansen. She died in 2001, 95 years old. My friend and also a physical therapist of my age, Gudrun Øvreberg (1986), continued her work and developed it further. I'm sure she would say, "I generated this together with the clients I met." She understood that sometimes we turn inward; we bend and close the body. We bend in the arms, close the hands, bite our teeth, and close our eyes. We creep together, to protect the front side of the body that is the feeling side of the body. All the feelings come on that side. What she did was to help people to stretch and open up. When she was able to do that, the feelings came back, and the words came back, and the colors came back, and the stories came back.

What she did was to cause a pain. She grabbed a muscle, for instance in the arm or in the cuff of the leg. When she grabbed that muscle, it produced pain. The body responds automatically with an inhalation, and when we inhale, we tend to stretch more. When we inhale more, we tend to stretch even more, and we take in air and we fill the chest. When the chest is filled and the air goes, for instance with a sigh, some of the tension in the body disappears. What she did was to help people to make bigger breathing movements. It's interesting to notice the metaphor in that she had to cause pain to bring more breathing. She always encouraged people by saying, "Let air come." She never said, "Breathe in"; she said, "Let air come." For me, that is the metaphor "Let life come." We all know that the first thing we do in life is to let air come, to let the spirit come. We take in the spirit; we let the spirit come. It is sacred. The last we do in life is to spirit out. Between that first spirit in and the last spirit out, it goes on all the time by itself, and we don't even notice it.

This strange woman, who impressed me enormously, was interesting when she tried to show the work to young physical therapists, as she got very irritated. During the break, she said, "Tom, they are so stupid, they don't understand anything."

I said, "That is because you tell them so abruptly, you tell something there, something here, something there, and you don't tell them what is in between. You speak incomprehensibly."

She said, "Do I?"

I said, "Yes, we have to write a book on it." Which we did: Gudrun Øvreberg and I wrote the book (1986).

She always wanted people to stand firmly on the ground. If the tension in the legs was too low, and they stood with poor balance, she first worked with the legs so they got strong, and so they could stand firmly on the ground. Then she let them lie on a bench and started to work from the legs up to the face, which is a very sensitive part of the body. When she was pulling the throat, stretching the muscles, her hands took care of the throat, and her eyes followed the breathing. If you look at her eyes, you can see how she follows the movements of the breathing. She was like an eagle, and those eyes were fantastic. Her eyes and her hands worked so well together.

She didn't need the thinking, and that reminds us of something Ludwig Wittgenstein (1953, p. 15) said: "When you are looking for similarities in different kinds of games, for instance chess or football or cricket, just see, don't think."

That's an extremely good thing for therapists to do: just to see, feel, and hear, not to think. When we wrote that book about her work and sent the manuscript back and forth, she read and made comments and she was very excited. She said, "This is so interesting. I have never known that I did this."

I said, "Yes, that's why we're writing the book." This lady had a profound impact on me. It was as if she filled me with uneasiness, the knowledge of just getting to see her made me restless. I used much of my life trying to understand what this woman was doing.

Her eyes told her hands how to work. Just see, don't think! I think working on the book, which started in 1983 and was finished in 1986, contributed to the change from "instead of" to "in addition to." If her hands were too soft or too weak or not producing enough pain, she could see that the movements of the breathing either did not change or stopped. She taught me to work on the sentence of Gregory Bateson, the famous sentence where he said, "A change makes a change." That is an active way of phrasing it. This lady made me change the words slightly to "A change is made by a change." It's more passive. If her hand was too soft, no change in the movement of the chest occurred. But if the hand was a bit stronger, it produced more movement of the chest. If her hand was too tough, or kept on too long, people made a big inhalation and did not let it go again. That was what she was looking for all the time. If the movement of the chest stopped, she immediately let her hand go.

I think this lady brought the big change from "either/or" to "both/and." Going from the perspective "either/or" to "both/and" gave the families the chance to stay alive. When we, in our scientific investigations, come to give freezing descriptions of people, these descriptions can easily freeze them. That could even happen in family therapy.

Reflecting Teams

An idea then came in the open that had been there from 1981. We worked the Milan way from 1978 to 1980. When we came down to the Milan group in 1981 to train with them, I thought, "Why do we leave the room when we should find out what to tell the family?" "Why don't we rather stay there and speak out loud so they can hear what we say?" "Maybe it would be helpful for them to see how we worked, not the outcome that we found, but how we came to it."

When that idea came, it was pushed aside as I was convinced that if we spoke in the open we would hurt them or we could humiliate them. Where did that idea come from? Certainly it came from how we spoke about the families in the closed rooms. We could say, "Oh, what a stubborn woman!" or "My goodness, think of living with such a talkative man!" One cannot say that in the open. So that idea, which definitely came from the closed rooms, prevented us from trying to take this out in the open for 4 years.

One day in March 1985, when we asked the family, "Would you like to listen to us for a while?" and they said, "Yes!" there was a new change. We spoke without being prepared; we just spoke. We did not come up with one comment for the group. We said very different things. I have learned that the power in such reflecting comments comes when we reflect on what we heard, which means reflect on what they said rather than reflect on what they did not say. It's so easy to sit and listen and start to think of what they said, and then reflect from what we think of what they said instead of just reflecting on what we heard. The best way is to first summarize what we hear before we reflect in a very questioning manner. The context of the reflection is what they said, because the moment we start to reflect from something we didn't hear, it loses its power.

Discussion I

Harlene: Very nice Tom, thank you. I was thinking about my own journey, as you were talking, and some of the similarities. What struck me was the whole idea of the client's voice and if you really listen to the client and you hear what they want you to hear, how different you are as a professional, as a therapist, and how different your therapy is. How much easier it makes your job. How much we can learn from the clients and from their wisdom.

 Then I was thinking about the ideas of "translation" and "interpretation." We are always in a process of translating and interpreting. We sometimes forget that, and we sometimes get too involved in paying attention to our own translations and interpretations. I think when you were talking about your journey, you were warning us about that, particularly when you referred to the notion of "see but don't think." When you see and think, you begin to bring in your pre-understandings and your own interpretation. Often when you translate and interpret, your misunderstanding is too great, and you lose the opportunity for the connection with the other person.

Michael: Yeah, and you talked about how easy it is to become indifferent. I think that's easy for all of us, and I think that you challenge the idea that we cannot do anything; you challenged that very powerfully. I think it's very easy for all of us to think that we're outside the system. We don't walk in the corridors of power, so what can we do? I think your response is that we can do a lot.

In your speech, there are echoes of what Paolo Freire was saying. Many of you would know Paolo Freire as a Brazilian activist, community worker, and teacher. The thing he was most concerned with at the time of his death was what he called the "neoliberal fatalism," or the new liberal fatalism among the people of the professions. It's people with a liberal critique of how things are, but with a kind of fatalism, a paralysis of will. We critique everything, but what can we do? There's nothing that can be done, because we don't have access to power, and I thought a lot about this in relation to listening to Tom. The sentiment of his work is that we can do a lot, and there are many gaps that we can find. We can step into those gaps and there is so much that we can challenge, and I was thinking about a lot of the ripples that have come from Tom Andersen's work. Tom has had a profound influence on the practice of not just family therapy, but psychotherapy internationally. Many of his ideas and some of the developments that he has put together in collaboration with others have been embraced, and a lot of these practices actually run against traditions, against taken-for-granted ideas and therapeutic practice. I would have enjoyed seeing a conversation between Tom Andersen and Paolo Freire, because I think this would have been very rich.

Tom: What helps you not to be indifferent?

Audience Participant: (shouting out) Listening to you.

Tom: No (laughs)...I mean in your life. What helps you not to be indifferent? We are not indifferent.

Michael: No, I'm not indifferent. I think a lot of things contribute to me avoiding indifference, even though there is so much, there's a port toward it. I think many of the people who confronted me contributed to that. I was thinking about a story, actually it's a story of a woman who confronted me. She was in a psychiatric institution, and she had a diagnosis of schizophrenia. She had had many admissions to the hospital, and these admissions for her were helpful, because it gave her a rest spot—it was like an asylum for her. There were some positive aspects to it. These admissions also put her back in contact with professional people, who were like a family to her, because she had no other family. But there was a complication and that had to do with the way her life was spoken about within the institution. It was diminishing of her. It was reducing of her.

She was having a dilemma about this. To her the psychiatric services were like an extended family, and she wanted asylum, she wanted time out. So how could she deal with what was happening in the context of asylum, with the diminishing or demeaning ways of speaking about her? She had this fantastic idea. She was quite a good pianist, and she'd made a CD of some of her music. She ran away from the hospital; no one knew where she went, and she came back with this CD and wanted the staff to play it, to listen to her music. They said, "Fine, fine, we'll listen to it."

She said, "Tomorrow I will ask you what it was like for you to listen to my music."

I think this is extraordinary. The next day she asked the staff members what they had heard in the music, and they began to relate to her very differently. I find that very inspiring.

If I think of times when I'm feeling a little bit overwhelmed or a bit desolate in response to what is happening out there in the world or the demeaning and the diminishing of people's lives, I often think about this story. I have a power and privilege that this woman didn't have, and yet she found a gap, a space, that she'd gotten into with her own personal agency and she challenged the ways in which she was being spoken about. I find this story very sustaining of me. I carry it with me, and I draw a lot from it, so I guess that's it. That's a small answer to a very good question.

Tom: Did the story of the piano woman bring restlessness or calmness?

Michael: Probably both, actually. Some restlessness to do more, but a calmness in knowing that these small acts can ripple up, they can make a difference, and they're very important.

Jaakko: There are, of course, many voices when listening to stories. The story Tom told aroused one voice that specifically was becoming bigger and bigger. It was connected to what Tom said, that he's speaking as a scientist. I started to listen to the story as a scientist because that's, for the most part, what I have been doing for the last 5 years. In the sciences I have been doing, I also have to give some very frozen descriptions of what we are doing. My way to try and find a solution is when, for instance, I'm writing a scientific paper, I want the patients' voices to become heard, not only figures and statistics and analyses. I think these were very important ideas, that Tom proposed—what I heard anyway—that a part of science should also include emotions, persons, and contexts.

It seems to be the case in psychiatry at the moment that the mainstream tries to be quite the opposite. They want to be a kind of generalization of something, to be neutral, to be objective. I think that if we lose the emotions and the persons, the science becomes a use of power, not only for our clients but also for ourselves. Therefore it was very refreshing to hear the story of a scientist who has emotions involved. I think what we as scientists, and any scientist, should do is to think more of the context, absolutely not being indifferent, but to think that the things we are doing have a big impact on many lives. That is a challenging task: how to move from frozen stories in science to stories that have meanings for ourselves, our work, and the people whose lives we are making research of.

Michael: May I ask you a question to clarify something? You talked about the importance of actually introducing a small difference.

Tom: Appropriate difference.

Michael: Yes, introducing a small difference in a conversation. If it's too big, people can feel...

Tom: That doesn't work.

Michael: Yeah. Yet if it's too small, there is no difference. You also spoke about just seeing and just hearing, and there seems a contradiction between these two ideas—just seeing, just hearing and not thinking, but on the other hand, introducing a small difference. Would you mind speaking to that apparent contradiction?

Tom: First of all, I think contradictions are very useful. They make me think I don't fully understand. I think that's very important. I used to think that contradictions were ongoing in the talk, and they go on all the time. Questions are very simple in that talk. "Is this the moment to raise the question, or should I wait some seconds more?" "Can I see the moment I shall give this question?"

I will come back to it later today, that when we talk, we speak first of all to ourselves. When I speak out loud to you, I first speak to myself and then I suddenly hear something that I haven't heard before. Most probably you will see that and give me a pause to think of what I just said to myself. I think that's a part of the way we work, that we give the others a chance to think of what they just said to themselves. I can see when a person is talking with himself or herself about what he or she just said. I think, "Now it's time, now it's time." I think you do the same. I think we have a big respect for process.

Jaakko: It's interesting that you used the word *see* and not *hear*.

Tom: I also say *hear*, but Wittgenstein is saying, "Just see, don't think." I would say, "Just see and hear." Harry Goolishian said, "Listen to what they really say, and not to what they really mean." Those are profound words. After this first shift from either/or to both/and, leaving the closed rooms, and letting families listen to us, more happened. We paid more attention to listening than before, so the balance between talking and listening changed. Being more of a listener gave us the chance to reflect more on "what is it to speak, what is it to be in speaking?" John Shotter, who is influenced by Wittgenstein (1953), used the words of Wittgenstein, "be in speaking"—the activity of speaking.

In the following interview, we are dealing with one word almost the whole meeting. This was in 1991 and in this small glimpse, the woman was in trouble, physically ill, and stayed in bed for a long time, but she could not call her family to ask for help. As you will hear, she is saying, "In our family we should be self-reliant; *independence* was the big word in our family." The way she spoke the words and expressed herself appealed to me strongly, so I decided to investigate the word more closely. Because words can be very painful to speak or very frightening to speak, one should be a bit careful. Therefore, I raised a couple of general questions about the word first. One question here is "Was independence spoken in the open or was it said implicitly?" She could easily reply, saying, "It was said in the open." I asked, "Should you be independent, or was it more independence in general?" She can reply easily, this time saying, "We should be independent." Then I asked her, "If you look into the word *independent,* what do you see?" As you will see, she feels uncomfortable and she starts to speak about loneliness.

Interview I

Woman: We were supposed to be self-reliant, you know, a certain amount of *self-reliance*, a big word for us.

Tom: Self-reliance? Independence?

Woman: Yes, *independence* was a very big word.

Tom: How was the term *independence* expressed; was it out in the open or was it implicit?

Woman: It was . . . verbally.

Tom: Verbally? Words in the family? That you should be independent or independence in general?

Woman: No, that we should be independent; they wanted us to be independent.

Tom: So after you got acquainted with the word and let it be part of yourself . . . what do you see in that word, when you look into the word *independence*?

Woman: I don't like it. I personally don't like that word very much.

Tom: What don't you like when you see into the word?

Woman: I see things . . . Well, talking about loneliness; it's so hard for me, I just . . . It's just something I try not to think too much of. I guess the word *independence* does mean standing alone, and to me that just kind of means being lonely, being alone. . . . That's one of the words that I dislike. . . . They used to talk about me as being independent, and I finally just said to them, don't use that word about me anymore, it's reinforcing something about me that I don't like. To me it means having to do everything myself, and I've always felt like it's been forced on me. What I'd like to do, for me, is just . . . I don't think independence is a virtue, I don't think so at all. It means standing alone to me, it means . . .

So we are back to seeing and when she said, "*Independence* is the big word in our family," it felt like a shade came over her face. The word had an impact on her. There was a link, a correspondence between the word and her reaction to it. I could see there was a correspondence, but I could not understand what it was, but she could. Then we are back to the thought that when we speak, we first of all speak to ourselves. When she said the word *independent,* she was brought back to the moment when she was independent. The word created a flashback, which she calls loneliness.

That became a clear tendency in my work, to listen to every word and to notice particularly those words that touched and moved the person, and then carefully try to see if the word can be investigated further by a couple of questions. I'm surprised how easily people accept those questions about the words that move them.

One woman spoke of peace very emotionally, and she was asked, "Is *peace* a big word or a small word?"

She said, "A very big word."

She was asked, "If you walk into the word *peace,* what do you see and hear?"

Without hesitation she said, "I'm going into a meadow and it's summer afternoon, and I hear music."

"Which music?"

"Mahler's second symphony."

"Which part of the symphony?"

"At the end when the choir comes so beautifully."

She was asked, "Who is with you listening to Mahler's symphony?" She was alone and started to cry. "Who should have been with you?" She knew. "If you brought a picnic basket, what would you have in that basket?" She knew what kind of food and wine and everything.

Words—Universes Traveling By

That has made me think that the words that travel by in millions have many meanings in them, even big stories, landscapes. This became the big interest in the beginning of the 1990s and with this physical therapy as the background, it gave me some assumptions about language. It's, in a way, simple but also is crucial in this work to listen to every word and to see how the words affect the other person. When this woman gets moved, we can see there is a connection. We don't understand what the connection is, but she understands. My experience is that of seeing a story move the other person, which touches me. The moment when all participants are moved is a good time to raise a question.

The first assumption is that language encompasses all kinds of expressions, and spoken words are only one of many expressions. Dancing is a part of language; so is screaming, hitting, painting, writing, cooking soups—those are all part of my definition of language. There are many other expressions. What they all have in common is that language is physical, a bodily activity.

The second assumption is that we need these kinds of expressions to find a meaning. For instance, we need words to describe another person. The descriptions we give of reality, for instance of another person, make it possible for us to relate to that person. It happens that we immediately make a description of the other person, which is so negative that you cannot talk with them. If many people had negative description of one and the same person, that person can easily be excluded. In order for us to include people, we have to work on our description to make it more positive.

The third assumption, which Harry Goolishian was very eager to say, "We don't know what we think before we have said it." He said, "We have to keep talking in order to find out what we think." The expression comes first, then the meaning.

Assumption number four is, as we saw in the preceding example, words are personal. They bring us back to experiencing something we have experienced before. The word *independent* brought this woman back to moments of being lonely.

Another important assumption is that when we express ourselves, we tell something about ourselves to others and ourselves. Expressions inform, but in my assumptions they do more. We become the person we become when we express the way we express ourselves. One very simple example is to deal with the verb *to be*. We so easily can say that grandmother is so kind. I try to avoid speaking to myself in that way. I rather say, "Grandmother is doing something kindly all the time, so she becomes kind." It's a difficult job to be kind. To become kind is very hopeful, as one can just start to do something kindly.

The other verb that is very dangerous to use without thinking it over is *to have*. To say, "He has a strong aggression" or "She has a deep depression" can have a strong forming effect on our ways of thinking about other people. "He HAS aggression," meaning he has it inside himself. Michael works so beautifully with such sayings. I used to ask the people who speak like that, "I can't see the aggression. Can you point it out to me?" If the person tried to tell me and I still could not see it, I'd say, "Please go and put your hand on it so I can see it more clearly." If that person got a bit embarrassed, I could ask, "Would you like me to say how I would express that?" If the person wants to hear that, I would say, "When this or that happened to the man, he got very angry." Or for a woman described as having a deep depression, one could say that when somebody said this or that to her, she got very sad and cried.

For me, I'm very eager to listen to my own speaking. Your willingness to listen to me gives me a chance to speak to myself, and I follow carefully what I hear. Through that, I can investigate my thinking. To listen to myself misusing the verb *to be*, I can freeze people. If I re-enter to become, I can make them alive again.

I have one last assumption about the practice of language that I will say a few words about. When I speak with people, I always take as a starting point something I heard. I never take as a starting point something I see, if what I see is not followed by a word. If a person looks like . . . you could say, "You look angry today." I strongly avoid speaking that way. It is safer to ask, "How are you today?" The person who looks very angry says, "I'm very happy today!" That gives me a chance to ask, "What makes you happy today?" I try to stick very closely to this. If there is a long-standing, very trusting relationship, as it can be between a wife and a husband, or between a mother and her son, maybe one could comment on what they see. I personally avoid it strongly in my professional life. I have heard that this rather strong statement provokes irritation, so I ask you to forgive me, but I stay with what I say.

We have so many words we use to talk to ourselves about human beings that our own speaking to ourselves can easily bewitch us. We are talking about personalities, characters, and psychological structures. So many words make us think that there's something inside us, where what we say and what we do is coming from. That's such a strong basic assumption in the Western culture. But Wittgenstein (1953, p. 129) is saying in the book I have referred to before, that the most important aspects of life we don't see, because they are lying just in front of us all the time. I will speak to what is just in front of us, without thinking.

When we hear the scream of the newborn, that scream is received by those who are there, and they make some hot water, and she is dipped in the hot water and she feels comfortable. That is, in a nut-shell, life for me. Her scream is an answer to the feeling of coldness. She has had it very warm and nice inside her mother, and she comes out into reality, which is a bit cold, and answers with a scream. The others receive the scream and answer by doing something. Her scream is her way of expressing herself. That is one thing that we depend on as human beings, having our expressions seen and responded to. That can often be a tragedy in Norwegian psychiatry. When patients in Norway have a psychotic expression, they are very often not received. Psychiatrists say, "These expressions are meaningless." In Western Lapland, they don't speak in such a way. They say, "Even if we do not understand the meaning in the expression, we will search for it." They receive it and give something back.

Discussion II

Jaakko: I started to think about the idea of why some expressions are not received. Why the expressions of a psychotic patient or these kinds of expressions, which move us, are not accepted. I think we professionals have the idea that we have to have control, and becoming emotionally involved often means a challenge to that control. We do not lose any control or we do not lose anything by doing it, but I have an assumption that it has a lot to do with the idea that we always have to have control, and some unpredictable things that are said are too big a challenge for that control.

Harlene: Yeah, but there are so many theoretical traditions that we've inherited, that are hard to shake.

Michael: There's a lot of unlearning for us to do. Within the context of this unlearning we can ask ourselves, what does it mean if we're not transparent? What does it mean if we obscure how these powerful encounters touch us? I believe that when we obscure this or that, we're marginalizing people who consult us; we are seeing them as "the other."

Tom, I'm very drawn to the ethics of your practice. Some of these descriptions, like "I challenge what I see, if it's not followed by a word." There are many examples like this that are illustrations of ethical practice, of the responsibility you take for the consequences of what you say and do in your conversations with people. I'm very interested in the words that you're drawn to, because you're drawn to certain words, which you then encourage people to unpack. Like *independence*: "Let's open that suitcase and unpack that word and other words that you're drawn to."

A piece that I find missing in your account of your work is that which informs the words you are drawn to. I'd be interested to hear your thoughts on why you're drawn to some words; it's not just the person's expression and what's in that expression. I don't think these words are just between you and the person. I think it is also about what resonances these words touch in you. You hear so many things that powerfully resonate for you in some way, that resonate with some of your own experiences. What interests me is how you speak about this without imposing something on a person. That's one of the pieces that I felt was missing.

Tom: I can feel pain myself when I see someone in pain. That's not their pain, it's mine. I call it sadness, but I think a better word is pain. I feel painful seeing people in pain, so . . . there was a man I met one month ago, he's 85 years old and he took part in a war. He was in a Nazi camp for 3 years and experienced awful things. He came home, where he lived with his sister who is 5 years older—she's now 90—and when he was taken by the Nazis and he was in prison for 3 years, his mother died.

He said, "When I came home in '45, my father was there and he had become a very, very old man." He had never spoken of what happened to him during the war. He determined shortly before he came, "Now I will take the chance." And he spoke and cried and then I asked him, "When you met your father in the railway station, what did he say?" and he cried very heavily and he could not find the words. I said, "Can you remember what you said to your father?" He cried and could not find the words. I said, "Maybe you did not speak, you only embraced each other, and did it like that without words." He was so much in pain, and it was very painful to see, so I think it has to do with that. My feeling must not come in the way of the other's expression. That is very important to me.

Michael: I understand that and believe the way you express this resonance is ethical. My sense is that you hear things that resonate with what you hold precious, with what you give value to. This shapes many of your responses.

Tom: Yeah... I have many thoughts during talk, which I don't share. I don't think it is necessary that everything should be told or said. I have to ask myself, "Maybe the person has had enough."

Harlene: That's what I was thinking Tom, seeing your work over time. If you don't feel a resonance, you let it go. When you were talking about the woman, you said, "I could see there was a correspondence. I didn't know what it was, but she did." You had a sense that the talking was important to her, and she had a sense that you were responding to her, that you were interested in her and trying to understand her. It seemed that it was very important to her. My guess is, had she signaled to you in any way that that was not the right connection, you would have let go.

Jaakko: I started to think of your conversation because I think it's a very good illustration of the very unfortunate thing, which often happened at the time I was practicing so-called systemic family therapy. There could be a team behind the mirror, especially if it was a training situation. There was a team or a supervisor; even I was in that role sometimes, looking from the outside, not sitting in the room and receiving this resonance. Then they would give comments that came from the outside, without the context or any possibility at all to share this feeling or to become emotionally involved. In my opinion, it's a very unfortunate way to use power, because, as you said, families get so easily slapped in that practice.

Harlene: Yeah, I think it's very different to be in the immediate emotional field, and I think the further you remove yourself from that, the more apt you are to draw from your own understandings and interpretations. In my work with people trying to learn to be a therapist, I think it's very important to have them experience being in a conversation from different positions, so they can experience what they're struck by, what they're drawn by.

Michael: Part of what I see you doing, Tom, is questioning so much, so that when someone says "I'm striving to be independent," you don't have this assumption that this is a path to psychological health. You don't routinely accept this. You ask questions about what is taken for granted all of the time. I'm wondering what you would say about how your questioning of "taking things for granted" makes it possible for you to interview someone about what independence means. You don't respond with "Okay, I'll help you get up to the correct end of the continuum of constructed normality, toward being more self-contained, more independent." Instead, you have these questions about what people routinely accept to be the truth. You challenge notions about what is authentic and what is not.

Tom: Well, when you said, "I'm striving to be independent," the way you said it, I think I would focus on the word *striving*, not on *independence*. I could have asked, "Have you been striving for a long time?"

Michael: But again, you are questioning the notion of striving, which is highly culturally valued. I just have a sense that it's your ability to critique culture and what is routinely accepted that opens up some of the possibilities for you in these conversations.

Tom: It comes very spontaneously. I'm sure the way you said striving, I would ask, "Have you been striving alone or with somebody?"

Harlene: I don't experience your questions as challenging a meaning that someone has for a word. I hear or experience them as you trying to learn more about their meaning, and in that inquiry or questioning you're engaging with each other and talking about it, which is a generative meaning-making process in itself. I don't see your intent as trying to challenge it or move it toward something else, but its shifting or moving toward something else is inherent in the kind of dialogical process that you invite with the other person.

Tom: The pause before they find the words is very important; the pause that comes after they have spoken, that's my job to protect. Don't make them disturbed. That's important. I see *protect* as a word I prefer to use when I think of them. We are there to protect, and we certainly protect everybody's dignity, that's number one.

Harlene: I was thinking of something Gregory Bateson said one time at a conference. He said, "I always like to have at least 7 seconds before I respond."

Tom: I used to say to myself, "Take one inhalation and one exhalation and one re-inhalation and one re-exhalation, then I can go on." That's my pause!

Our Work as Therapists

I will try to start to summarize how I see our work as therapists. I have been very interested in finding forms to take all kinds of knowledge into consideration. These kinds of knowledge are the feeling part: the experience in the body as when we feel pain, seeing the other person in pain, and also comprising understanding of what it might be. And lastly explaining what it is.

I will propose a very simple procedure to work out these few things. I will let you read a small interview about a man who is often very irritated, is a bit suspicious, and also used too many drugs, and the HIV virus has infected him. He is coming to the therapist to talk. The therapist is Joan DeGregorio in New York, who is a student of Peggy Penn.

This gives us also a chance to let you know a bit about Peggy Penn's work. Peggy is also very occupied with language and she's occupied with three different kinds of voices that are parts of us. The first voice we develop is the social voice we use with other people; the many social voices we use in the art of social talk with others.

The next we develop is the voice to ourselves, as small children use when they are sitting and playing to themselves, talking loudly. The words in that talk are as important as the hand when it comes to the play they are engaged in. Then, around the time we start school, there comes a third kind of voice. That is the inner voice, and we have a lot of inner voices; voices that come in pairs and often oppose each other. The physical therapist learns that in the body, we have two sets of muscles: those that bend and close the body, and those that stretch and open it up. The reason I'm standing in balance, not falling, is that the stretchers on the front of my knee and the bending muscles on the backside are active at the same moment; the same in the hip.

That metaphor goes also with inner voices. Peggy thinks that sometimes one of the voices gets dominant and marginalizes other voices. She encourages people to write a letter to somebody. Bill is the name of the man; he's sitting to the left. His wife, Ann, is sitting to the right. He is very angry with his father. He said, "Had my father been different, my life would have been different." His father was very much away and when he came home, he drank heavily, so he was away also then, sort of. "Had my father been different, my life would have been different." This is a very strong angry voice. Peggy will never try to control that voice, but rather encourage the opposite voice to grow.

Interview II

Bill (reading a letter): "... brave, I've never really enquired about you to Mom, and I've never called Barry, your friend and best man, to call and talk about you, because I've never really cared." (cries) "But you know what, Dad, writing this letter tonight makes me realize that it's important to let myself feel love for you. I've been denying that for so long." (cries)

Joan: It's okay.

Bill: Just got one more sentence. "I'm sure you did the best you could and for that I love you. Until we meet again, your son, Bill." (cries) I was worrying through the course of the day; will I be able to feel anything? Cause a lot of times I just wonder where are my feelings, they don't seem to be there, I feel nothing. And I can honestly say it was the first time I've ever felt any kind of love for my father, writing that last night. And then when I felt that, I thought, "God, that's a strange thing," you know? And then I recognized how necessary that is, you know, to go through that feeling.

In the next little interview, Bill is present, Ann is present, Joan, and myself. We are four people. We are looking back on the therapy that we were doing before. This is a way to investigate what goes on in therapy. I say in the beginning that we are here to investigate the collaboration you did together, back in time. I say to Bill and Ann, "Joan invited you and she invited me to come so we are the guests and she is the hostess. We had the chance today to investigate the collaboration we did from two different perspectives, from the therapist's perspective, Joan's, and the client's perspective, which is yours. Since Joan is the hostess, I will start to speak with her, would you listen to that for a while? Then I will speak with you and let Joan listen to that."

I didn't say it here, but this is a way that we can reach all three different kinds of knowledge: the knowledge we feel in the body, which has been called "tacit knowledge" and which John Shotter calls "knowledge of the third kind"; the other knowledge, which is understanding what it might be; and the last kind, which is explaining what it is. My job as an outsider, which I call myself, is to be on the "how" level. "How did you work together?" I must not go into asking "what" questions. If they want to talk more about what happened between them, or difficulties or things like that, I would say, "I understand there's more to talk about, so I withdraw and you talk with Joan." It's very important to me to stay on a "how" level.

I'll summarize first what Joan told me, so I summarize the words. They made small steps, important steps, made discoveries, and so on. Then we talk a bit about that before the couple says how it was for them.

Interview III

Tom: And you said the discoveries were comfortable...you said that...I think those were some of the words you used...and the discoveries you made to get it to work very comfortably, what did you do in the work with those who were there to make it comfortable and to make it possible to discover...what is comfortable?

Joan: Comfortable is for me as a therapist...is to create an atmosphere for your clients that will allow them to just be, to talk about whatever it is that they need to talk about, and that you as a therapist are going to hold it, that it's not going to make you uncomfortable, that it's not going to turn you off. Whatever it is, you can hear it and you can hold it. (pause)

Ann: Persistent...you are a persistent conscience. I think it's good for us in general, because she brings up the things that we don't like to talk about, or we want to, but we don't want to. And she is that nudge, the nudge in the side that kind of gets the ball rolling.

Tom: So that's good for the talk that she should be persistent.

Ann: Yes. Yeah.

Tom: Do you have the common experience?

Bill: Yes, she's a fine...really fine, and genuine person, and the fact that she's so patient with us to let us just ramble along, and she recognized that as important, just to listen. A very good listener. And good timing also. Things just seemed to work out with all of us. There was a good, good bond of trust with Joan. It's definitely that we've been playing with. It's not like therapist–client, not at all.

It's on a very even field. And she's a real person, she cares about what she's doing, and you have to have that emotional connection; it makes a big difference. When I read that letter here, I could see a tear in her eye. And that meant so much to me, like she could feel what I was going through. That strengthened the bond. She's a real person, you know, no pretension.

Tom: If you might find more words for a real person, what would those words be? What does a person do that is a real person?

Bill: She listened real well, and sort of gave you a lot of hope, let you . . .

Ann: Make you feel comfortable, and I mean that the more we learned about Joan, the easier it was for us to reveal more of ourselves too. We learned Joan is a mother, she has children around our age, she's Italian, she believes in all this family stuff, and I could identify with that. So that when I was having difficulties, like working through some family holiday problems that we always have, I trusted her judgment.

Tom: Good.

Ann: So it helped, yes.

Tom: So knowing something about her background was useful?

Bill: Absolutely.

Tom: Know something about her identity . . . ?

Ann: It helped, yeah; it helped develop a little floor.

Bill: It was very important, yeah, to make her a real person, to have that background and family and all the little things. Our table was set?

Ann: And yet be so far away that we could see her as being objective, you know, not being involved.

The information that comes out of this is very local. This is knowledge for Joan. Probably it fills her, in this case, with joy, which will encourage her to work in the same way with others. In other meetings, the family or the couple can tell things that make the therapist think, "I must do it differently"—the kind of knowledge that fills them with uneasiness. They cannot get peace before they change their style. So that's a small attempt to reach all three kinds of knowledge in the same meeting.

Discussion III

Tom: You don't need to ask questions; you can come up with opinions, strong opinions, protests.

Question: I was reflecting on some of your earlier thoughts when you talked about your philosophy being generated from a cultural flow. You talked about the flow of solidarity and how you stop yourself from being too political in this process. Is your process, the work you do, a political process? If it is a political process of solidarity, how do you avoid leading clients down your particular ideas and your particular thoughts? Does that make sense?

Tom: Yes. I don't know what to say. I think networks work is very political. It is to restore solidarity, which is very political. Privatization is the opposite, and it has a very short history. Reagan, who is to be buried the day after tomorrow, he and Thatcher started it 30 years ago, and it has had an enormous rapid impact. And that's very political, to privatize. I want solidarity to be brought back.

Audience: The reason why I asked this question is because I've been working in Northern Ireland, in Belfast, with two very different communities: one Protestant and one Catholic. I'm also English, which creates some issues for me because of the history of my country in terms of how it's treated the people of Ireland. Each of these two communities has its own history, its own pain and suffering, and I struggle sometimes with balancing the two perspectives and working with some community work as I'm on both sides of the divide. I wonder sometimes how I balance that; it's not always very easy to do.

Tom: That was a comment; that was not a question.

Audience: It was just an observation, a comment. If you wish to comment on it, you can. Or perhaps any of your colleagues may want to do that.

Tom: I have a comment. In situations where two opposing forces are active at the same time ... one part of a person that is hitting badly ... I try to search for an opposite part of the person, which they always have. Every person has a

good side, so when one becomes dominant, it's important to bring the other part forth. Then do not encourage
the one part to dominate the other part. I think that was
one of the things that Bush and his Republican friends
did wrong. Both voices should be heard—Islamic voices,
Christian voices—and not let one dominate the other.
When a person comes up and you can find that part of the
person that says, "I don't want to hit," and the other voice
says, "I want to hit," let them be side by side. That's peace
work for me. So I see therapy as peace work. So God bless
your work in Belfast.

Audience: Thanks.

Audience: Hello. I have a question about the last interview. I would
just like to ask about... I'm working with couples and
working by myself and not having a therapist by my side,
so I was wondering, can the reflection be used so that the
couple can reflect the work of the therapist to the therapist?
In that interview, you were... there was the couple and the
therapist and you were there with them. If you were just the
couple and the therapist, can you ask the couple to talk with
each other and to reflect on how the therapy is going?

Tom: I think that's possible.

Audience: I was wondering how you see that... what would be the
benefit? Is it a very selfish benefit to ask the couple to talk
about how the therapy is going just to get some information,
or is it... did you understand what I was asking?

Tom: Not fully.

Audience: Well umm... is there any benefit for the couple to reflect the
work of the therapy to the therapist? Do you understand now?

Tom: Yes. Well, I think there is a difference. Everything can work,
but in this case, when I speak with the couple, Joan had two
possibilities: to keep her ears open or to close them. That's
not so easy when the couple is talking straight to you, you
must listen to it. He or she has the possibility not to listen.

Audience: Yeah, I understand.

Tom: That's the main difference. But everything is possible. Can you
try it and write me and tell what happened?

Audience: Do you think it would be beneficial?

Harlene: If you followed Tom's idea that we are as researchers, the everyday clinician as a researcher, and insider versus outsider research, and if you continually invite your client to reflect on "How are we doing?" "Is this helpful?" "Are we moving in the direction you want to move in?" and continually invite their reflections with their feedback, then you fine-tune together what you're doing as you go along. This is very different than a reflective conversation at the end of therapy. I think what you're asking about can be extremely valuable. In all of my work with learners at the Houston Galveston Institute, that is what we talk about with them all the time. We continually reflect with clients to invite their reflections on the question, "How are we doing together?" and use that conversation again as a part of "fine-tuning" and developing the next step.

Audience: I've been thinking about this idea of how to keep the idea as a therapist that people are multivoiced or multistoried. As a therapist, I think it's sometimes quite difficult to see . . . keep the idea that our clients are multivoiced, multistoried. What helps me to really keep in my mind that there are lots of different stories?

Michael: I think that's an important question, because it's about the development of our skills in being able to recognize the traces of the other stories or voices, and I think that's a skill we're all working on. I'm constantly working on this. How do I identify those thin, latent traces of the other stories of life or other voices of identity? I think this is one of the most important questions that we could ask ourselves.

I am now thinking about a family that I saw not so long ago, in a workshop context. A young man of 15 years of age was in trouble with a number of agencies and authorities. He had a diagnosis of Oppositional Defiance Disorder. It was his parents' idea to bring him to this consultation, and he was not happy to be present. In fact, he seemed quite resentful about being in this context. I asked him about the circumstances of his presence, and he told me he was dragged along. Although he had been fully informed about the context, he then said in a highly antagonistic voice, "Who are these people anyway?"

In the early part of our meeting, all of this young man's responses could have been read as the verification of the diagnosis of Oppositional Defiance Disorder. However, addressing the question "What might these responses reflect in terms of his initiatives?" positioned me to play a part in identifying a subordinate storyline of this young man's life. I asked him what he would like to know about the people present and, surprised by this question, he said he wanted to know about their hobbies. I interviewed all of the workshop participants about their hobbies. When I eventually got back to the young man I asked what he heard that had caught his attention. He talked about what he'd related to in these stories about the participants' hobbies, and I asked him to name the step he had taken in the meeting in relating to the workshop participants in this way. He said he didn't know, so his mother offered, "He was building bridges and we haven't seen this for 5 years." The young man then verified that this was the case, and this opened the door to a re-authoring conversation. Even the very expressions of life that are taken up in a confirmation of some deficit construction can also be understood to be an initiative of some sort. I find this a very helpful idea!

Tom: If a person speaks of pain or something else, ask the person, "If that pain found a voice, what would it say?" to make the voice speak. Then ask, "Who do you want to receive that voice, and how will the other person respond?" To make everything speak, think of where it should be received and what the response would be. There are so many bits in a talk, where we can search for voices. If there's a good person in that person's life, you could then ask, "If your grandmother were here, what would she say about how we talk?" We bring a strong, big network with us, which Jaakko is very much into. Bring not only the network that is out there, but also a network in here—even a network of foreign voices, which sometimes are called psychotic symptoms. John Shotter makes this distinction. He doesn't talk about speech but speaking. Words are to reach out to be connected. Words are like hands that try to make a handshake.

A Meeting Before the Meeting, Then the Meeting

This happened in Finland. It was a part of a local, 3-year training program. Jaakko Seikkula has written extensively from his own work (Seikkula, 1995; Seikkula, Alakare, & Aaltonen, 2001a, 2001b, 2001c; Seikkula, Alakare, & Haarakangas, 2001). It was the team of three that wished a family they were working with to come, and they wanted me to be active in the talk that 50 trainees and trainers in the audience should follow. The room was an amphitheater in a beautiful local library.

First I asked, as I usually do, "Is there something you want to say before the family comes, or can we wait until they are here?"

One person in the team said, "There were many families we could have chosen between, but we picked this particular one," and another continued, "because we in the team are occupied with the fact that many in the family have been psychotic. We are uncertain how we shall understand that in relation to this case. Maybe it is hereditary that the daughter does not want to go to school and has dropped drivers training and will not be friends and most probably hears voices."

My comment was then, as so often, a question and was based on the thought that maybe the family already has enough concerns and should be released from having the team's concern in addition to their own.

"If the family had been here, how would it be for them to hear a discussion among us about the team's concerns?" The team said we should wait for the family. I hinted that maybe the family's presence and participation were not necessary for the discussion of the team's concerns.

Before the family came, I asked the translator if she had any preferences for the translation. She had not, and I thought that I have had the same answer all over the world; translators are extremely flexible. Usually families prefer to speak for a while and have that summarized. I told the translator to give the family the time they needed and "you summarize it your way." "Do it the way you feel comfortable with." "Correct translation is not necessary."

It is important that the person in the family that speaks can *see* that the person who hears the words also receives them. As long as I do not understand the local language, I cannot be that person. It is good if the translator, as much as possible, takes the therapist's position (in this case mine).

A mother and her 19-year-old daughter entered the auditorium, high up in the back, and walked slowly down to the stage that was deep down in the front of the room. The mother, Sara, was very concentrated and almost did not notice the attendants. It felt like she was very preoccupied with something. It was as if it was written in her eyes: I have brought an agenda with me, and I need help!

The daughter, Maria, followed the mother carefully and saw and copied what the mother did. They sat down close to each other. The mother sat with her legs side by side, and one hand embraced the other hand; the one hand rested in the other hand. They did not squeeze each other. The daughter had her legs crossed. The arms shifted between being crossed and uncrossed, and one hand was searching to her mouth.

I excused myself for not being able to speak their language and had to be helped by a translator, and asked: "How would you like to have the translation?" They did not understand, so I said, "Do you want the translation word by word, or is it better to talk for a while and have it summarized?" They wanted sentence by sentence and that was okay with the translator.

I asked, "Would you like to know more about me than what you have been told"?

The mother said: "Why are you here, and where are you coming from?"

I said that I had had a long collaboration with those who work here and that they wanted me to come to their training program, that I had been there before and that they come to Tromsø where I work at the university. I noted, "We had a short meeting before you came. Would you be interested to know what I was told?"

They wanted to. I said that they were selected as the one family to come, from among many others, and that I had heard that Maria's father had been a psychiatric patient, that the team was occupied by that, and I had said to the team, maybe we could have a meeting about that issue without the family present. I had also been told that Sara was divorced from Maria's father 10 years ago, and that Maria, at the moment, neither preferred to go to school nor train for car driving, nor be with her friends and that Sara is concerned about that. Sara responded to this orientation by saying, "I am so glad to be here."

Her hands opened carefully and were lying side by side, and she said that many relatives had been to the psychiatric hospital: Maria's father's mother and also Maria's father's mother's father. Maria's older sister Marta and their father's brother had been in similar situations. This uncle committed suicide.

I asked if she had more children, and she said that Johanna was her oldest daughter from a previous marriage. I asked, "Where is Johanna now?"

"I am not sure; she uses drugs and she is on the streets in a nearby city."

"When was the last time you saw her?"

"Three years ago."

Sara became divorced when Johanna was 3 years old, and Johanna was taken care of by her father and father's mother, and Sara was not allowed to see her daughter.

"Do you think Johanna has missed you during these years?"

"Yes!"

The hands found each other again, and she looked intensively at the translator and me.

"Have you missed her?"

"Yes."

Her eyes filled with tears, and she looked intensively at us.

"She has written to me and asked if she could come to us, to come home. Her father would not see her any more. But I am afraid that my two other daughters might start using drugs."

(To Maria) "When was the last time you saw your sister?"

"Three years ago."

"Do you miss her?"

"A bit."

"So both of you miss her?"

Both nodded, and Maria did not know where she should keep her hands. One hand searched first toward her mouth and then came back to the other hand. I said,

"It sounds like Johanna is lonely?"

Sara nodded and looked intensively at us, her hands held each other firmly.

". . . and I thought maybe you feel lonely yourself?"

"I have so much pain!"

There came quietness in the room and a pause, and I asked, "Where in your body is the pain"?

"In the heart and in the thoughts."

After a long quiet pause, I asked, "If your pain found a voice, what would it say?"

"It would scream!"

"With words or without words?"

"Without words!!"

She looked intensively at us as if her eyes said, "Help me!"

"Who would you like to receive your scream?"

"God."

"How should God respond to your scream?"

She now kept her hands tight together and said she hoped God could take care of her three daughters. There came a long pause, and it was very quiet in the room. Nobody made the smallest movement. Everybody seemed very moved, including the translator and me.

I asked the three in the team what they had been thinking. The second therapist had been thinking of the possibility of Maria hearing voices, and I asked, "Would it be more interesting to know more about that instead of what Sara just said?" The therapist became uncertain and could not find an answer. The third therapist said that she was very moved by what she heard of Johanna. She had never heard that before. Sara had, at this point, crossed her legs and her hands were on the knees as she listened intensively.

I asked if Sara had had a chance to think to the future. As her hands grasped each other again, she said she was very worried about the future.

"Do you have any adult to turn to and talk with?"

" No."

"Do you have a mother or a father to talk with?"

No, her father died when she was 3 years old, and the new man she married shortly afterward did not want Sara's mother to be with her.

"So, maybe you also have felt lonely?"

She said, "My daughters are all I have," and cried quietly, and there came a big silence in the room. Maria had at this moment lifted one hand to her mouth; did she try to say something? I asked if somebody sometime had been close to her—somebody who was close and understood her? Father's mother and father's father had; in their presence she felt understood and protected. They both died when Sara was a teenager.

"If they were here now, they might help you?"

"Yes," she cried silently and looked down at her hands.

In these moments I have to consider all the time if it is too difficult for her to talk; if that were the case I would pick another issue, something easier to talk about. According to the impressions I received, I determined to continue, "They would maybe have understood your worries and pain and fear for the future?"

"Yes."

"If they had been here, maybe you did not have to scream to God?"

"No."

Her tears were streaming. "If your grandmother had been here, what would she have said?"

"Little girl, you have been so good to your daughters!"

"What would you say back?"

"Grandmother I love you so much!"

"And what would she then do?"

"She would put her arms around me, and I could smell her. She smells so good!"

Many in the audience wept silently.

"Maybe you could bring them a bit back to your thoughts; maybe that would make it better?"

"It feels less painful when I speak of them!"

(To Maria) "Would you like to say what you have been thinking?"

"I have understood that my mom has had pain, but she never said anything. I did not know anything about her grandparents."

"How would it be for you if your mother took you to their grave and also told a bit about them?"

"That would be good."

"Was it better to hear about your mother's pain or would it be better not to hear?"

"It was better to hear."

"Maybe your mother would protect you and your sister from hearing about her pain and fear for the future?"

"Yes, maybe."

When Sara was asked how it had been for her to be there, she said it was good for her to have a listening audience.

"Maybe you and Maria would like to hear what they have been thinking?"

Both did, and I turned to the audience and encouraged them to talk to me. That would be better for the team and for the family. If the audience talked with me, the team and the family could choose either to listen or let their mind go to other places if that felt best. If the audience talked to them or looked at them when they talked, the team and the family would be forced to listen to them and could not let their mind travel to other places.

The first three persons said they had been very moved by Sara's consideration for the daughters. I asked if there was a grandfather's voice in the audience, and a man said it had made a big impression on him that Sara, despite her own pain, had so many thoughts for her daughters.

"Is there a grandmother's voice present?"

A white-haired woman said, "When I listened to this conversation I thought of a visit I made to my daughter and granddaughter yesterday; I thought how important it is for my granddaughter to have a mother, as it is for her mother to have a mother."

I felt that the meeting was close to a natural end; an outsider as me shall not "open" too much. It was important that the team and the family found their natural way to continue. Both Sara and Maria took their farewell with firm handshakes and firm looks.

Sara said, "And it was important to have a commenting audience."

The following week, Sara and Maria said the talk had been very useful but hard because it was painful. Maria had thought in the talk that it might be too much for the mother and she had thoughts about stopping it. The mother said it was not *too* much. They all thought that Maria should start school again. One in the team wrote this letter 3 months later:

> Dear Tom,
> I met Maria and Sara last week. They both are well. Maria doesn't have any psychotic fears or voices anymore. She can meet friends and wants to go to school in August. They send greetings to you. Be well and have a nice summer.
> B.

Afterthoughts

Since the pain had been brought to the open, perhaps one could, on a later occasion, hear if Sara's grandparents could conform in more ways. In her pioneering work, Peggy Penn often encourages those she meets to write a letter (Penn, 1994, 2001). She would maybe have asked Sara to write a letter to her grandparents and told her to bring the letter with her to their next meeting and read it out loud. Peggy Penn would most probably have also asked Sara to write a return letter from the grandparents to herself. This might have brought the voices of the grandparents to Sara's inner talks, and these voices might balance the voice of pain and the voice that feared the future.

Sara's expressed fear for the future could be a starting point for this: "I understand that there is a part of you that fears the future. If that part of you found a voice, what would it say?" During the "investigation" of that question, it is important to go slow and be sure that Sara, when she speaks, is always moved by her own words. If she is not moved by her own words, one should not proceed. If she becomes moved, one would continue: "Is there another part of you that has other thoughts or feelings or hope about the future?" If she confirms, one could ask: "If that part of you found a voice, what would it say?" When the two voices, which hopefully will balance each other, are heard, one could say, "A voice needs a home to stay; if a fearful voice should be put in your body, where should it be?" In the same way, the other voice is given a home. What seems to be very important is that the therapist does not take a side with one of the voices and not with the other, neither encourages the one voice to control the other voice. It is important that they can live side by side as in every peace work.

Closing Comments

The team offered their concern for their participation in the meeting. Sara offered her intensive presence. What shall one select to start from? Usually when all are present at the start, it is helpful to ask all how they want to use the meeting. Everybody has a chance to respond, and all answers are remembered as correctly as possible. When all have responded, one at a time, one goes back to the person who responded first and lets that person talk about what she or he wants to be heard. Then speak with the person who responded as number two, and so on. In this case the team responded first in the family's absence, and I asked myself when Sara and Maria entered the room, which expression—the teams or Sara's—is pressing the strongest? I chose to answer myself: Sara's.

In the work mentioned here, it was important first to find out with the team and the family how we should collaborate before we started the collaboration. The thoughtfulness about the "other" must come before the thought of what the other is. This is a bit of a "Levinasian" idea. Emmanuel Levinas's thoughts are, in a very fascinating way, written about in a Norwegian essay (Kolstad, 1995). When Levinas opened a door for the "other," he said, "Après vous!" and then he commented on that gesture by saying, "This is my philosophy." He preferred to put the philosophy of ethics before the philosophy of ontology.

When Sara talked, it was very important to listen to every word she said *and* to see how her own expressions touched and moved her. She searched after and found those expressions that helped her to find a meaningful step from the one moment to the next. Harry Goolishian constantly reminded us, "Listen to what they really say, and not to what they really mean!" In the moment we listen to what they really mean, we interpret what they say in our own perspective, which means that we make our meaning of what they say. For the listener, being therapist or researcher, it is important to throw out the inner voice that says, "What is he really meaning?" or "What is she trying to say?"

There is nothing more then what they say. So, we have to listen carefully to what they say.

My wish is at the moment that we stop talking about therapy and research as human techniques, and rather talk of it as human art; the art to participate in the bonds with others. If we exclusively started to use the term *human art*, how would that bewitch our understanding and our lives?

It has been of the utmost significance for me to think of the work that is sketched in this chapter as being fully based on practical experiences (*empiri*) where the most important aspect has been to find a way of collaboration where all participants are protected against having their integrity and identity humiliated. When that way of collaboration is found, time has come for the "theories," which I, in this chapter, have preferred to mention as assumptions.

International Outsider Thoughts

John Gurnaes: What first caught my attention was Tom's talk about "the road of indifference." "We must not be indifferent," he says. I think this is what his work is about—that is, finding ways to stay with others as well as with his own expressions of life and to be moved by them and respond to them, no matter what. "Just let life come," says Tom Andersen. "Stay with it, be moved by it and respond."

It seems that Tom's words, "Listen to every word and see how it affects the other person," have very clear implications in therapy. This is in line with Harry Goolishian's words, "Listen to what they really say, and not to what they really mean." These words were a message to therapists to move away from the hermeneutics of suspiciousness, to move away from looking "behind" or "under" a person's expression to reveal what the person's expression really means. In the field of family therapy this was a move away from the interpreting of family members' expressions as something that served a certain function in the system or were a surface manifestation of hidden structures in the family where the real meaning of the expression was to be found and which

the therapist had to reveal. This move away from the hermeneutics of suspiciousness meant, and still means, that therapists have to step away from their own interpretations and
theories, or to be "irreverent" to their own prejudices, as
Gianfranco Cecchin put it, and stay with the client's expressions. To me this is clearly the path Tom is on.

Tom says, "Listen to every word and see how it affects
the other person." He continues, "When this woman gets
moved, we can see there is a connection. We don't understand what the connection is, but she understands. Words
are very personal. They bring us back to experiencing something we have experienced before, as well as it connects us
to our expressions, feelings, and knowledge." About his
practice Tom says, "That became a very clear tendency in
my work, to listen to every word and notice particularly
those words that touched and moved the person, and then
carefully try to see if the word can be investigated further
by a couple of questions." As far as I can see, Tom's questions are questions that intend to connect a person's expression back to their experiences, relationships, and feelings.
This is to make sure that the small shifts and moves toward
something else in the conversation come from the person.
In this way, what connects the person to his or her life is
not lost. By doing this, I think, Tom stays very close to
his own words, "That is one thing we depend on as human
beings, having our expression received and responded to."
As I understand his work, this means that responding to
a person's expression in therapy is to give it back in a form
that connects the person to his or her expression, and not in
a form that alienates the person, takes the person away from
his or her expression, or moves the therapeutic conversation
into a monologue.

Something else also came to my mind while reading Tom's talk. It took me back to my first reading of
Wittgenstein's arguments about private language and
meaning in *Philosophical Investigations*. What Wittgenstein
says about private language is that it is an expression. Our

language about ourselves is not a statement that is either true or false but an expression and, in that way, connected to our life. This is very much in line with, I think, Tom's thinking about language. It challenges the popular idea in therapy that it is about achieving "insight" or "self-knowledge" about who we really are underneath what we think we are. Such an idea in therapy is founded in a representationalistic or naive-realistic understanding of language. According to this view, language is something that either represents or does not represent what it refers to in the outer world.

In therapy, this representationalistic idea about language has been taken up and directed toward our inner world in a way that opens up the idea that we can have true or false knowledge about a thing called "self." This self is a thing populated with entities, forces, and mechanisms like strengths, weaknesses, motives, character resources, conflicts, defense mechanisms, and so on. The idea was, and still is, that certain technologies and certain privileged therapeutic practices could provide us with access to knowledge about our inner world and ourselves. Wittgenstein's rejection of private language as a representation of our inner world short-circuits that idea as well as the meaning of therapeutic traditions founded on such an understanding. Our language about our self is an expression, and expressions are neither true nor false. But there is more to this.

In *Philosophical Investigations*, Wittgenstein argued against the representationalistic and naive-realistic idea of language as a kind of mystical connection between the "outer" and "inner" world. Wittgenstein spoke against the ideas that words and the world are connected, and that words got their meaning because of this connection in the beginning of time through a mystical baptism. Words and meanings are not something given over to us from the world. Language is our own invention in our daily life and the meaning of a word is simply how it is used in language.

So the primary relation of language is not to the world but to our practice, to our life form. Words like *strengths, weaknesses, motives, character, resources, conflicts,* and *defense mechanisms* are our own inventions. The ways we use them in our daily life give them meaning. Wittgenstein's understanding of language completely changes the understanding of what happens when people in therapy "achieve knowledge about themselves, about who they are." Tom's words, "We become the person we become when we express the way we express ourselves," express this change.

What really caught my attention in Tom's work is that he almost brings a Wittgensteinian understanding of language into therapy. By this I mean that he has left what I have called a representationalistic and naive-realistic understanding of language in therapy. Tom seems, as Wittgenstein does, to understand our language as connected to practice or life form. Wittgenstein says, "To picture for yourself a language is to picture for yourself a life form." What he means by this is that language is connected to our life form, to our expressions, our practices of life, our experiences, our relationships, our feelings, imaginations, as well as to our culture. Meaning is, in Wittgenstein's term, simply our use of words, which is to connect words to other words. Wittgenstein reminds us that the primary relation of language is not to the world or to the language itself, but to our practice or life form in which we use our language. So if the use of language in therapy is not connected back to client's life form—that is, to client's experiences, relationships, feelings, and other expressions of life, as well as to culture—it is simply just "meaning making out of the blue," which leaves clients untouched. Thank you, Tom, for bringing me to this track and sorry if I, in my eagerness, have taken your work and thinking too far away from what you recognize as your own expression.

Yishai Shalif: One of the many things that resonated for me was a short interchange between someone in the audience and Tom. The person asked whether Tom's work was political, especially with regard to the process of solidarity. The person in the audience was working in North Ireland and struggling to balance the two perspectives of the communities in conflict. Tom commented on the person's comment saying, "When one part of the person that is hitting badly...I try to search for an opposite part of the person.... Every person has a good side, so when one becomes dominant, it's important to bring the other part forth. Then do not encourage the one part to dominate the other part...both voices should be heard—Islamic voices, Christian voices—and not let one dominate the other. When a person comes up and you can find that part of the person that says, 'I don't want to hit' and the other voice says, 'I want to hit,' let them be side by side. That's peace work for me. So I see therapy as peace work."

This expression evoked an image of a choir with different voices each singing different notes. As someone who tries sometimes to harmonize, I'm aware of the difficulty to keep your own voice and not meld into the other voices singing different notes. The harmony is created from this variety of notes sung together, "side by side." This resonated in my life because harmony in general and the commitment to multivoiced "reality" are very dear to me. My son has just turned 13, and since this is the age when a Jew becomes obligated in the commandments, it is the Jewish tradition to celebrate this date (Bar Mitzvah). We had a reception for a few hundred people. One of the things that made me very happy and proud was the variety of different people. People were from the spectrum of religiosity, political affiliation, ages, and professions. This is not a taken-for-granted thing in Israeli society.

These words of Tom also brought to mind a conversation I had a few weeks ago with a young man of 17 who took part in the opposition and resistance to the Israeli army uprooting the Jews living in Gaza strip. He was very angry with the soldiers, policemen, politicians, and his own leaders for not being more militant. He told me of violent action of his during the uprooting; however, without me having to mediate he said, almost in the same utterance, that he would not do what other youngsters did. He would not abuse the soldiers and policemen verbally. "I will not give them a trauma," he said in his own words. "I lost my father in a terrorist attack and know what trauma is, I will not afflict it on others." I found myself allowing both voices to be expressed side by side without having to make one dominate the other.

I feel that the ability to make space for these opposing voices to be expressed and heard is an expression of a deep belief that the person himself will make peace between these voices. Tom's deep respect that is pointed out in different parts of his presentation is a great inspiration for working with people. Allowing for the variety of social voices, our own voices, and our inner voices (Peggy Penn's work) to be expressed in a side-by-side way is peace work. I'll be even more aware of the "side-by-side" peace work in the work I do in transforming listening between opposing groups in Israeli society; I'll be even more aware of this "side-by-side" peace work.

Tom's Response

Tom: I find Yishai's comments very striking, since he comes from a context where he has felt the uneasiness of oppositions and disagreements and even violence on and in his body. It is good to feel that my words found a place in his context. I became very glad when I read his comments.

I became also very glad when I read John's comments. When he referred to Wittgenstein, I felt he had grasped the Wittgensteinian context, and he found my words illustrating some Wittgenstein points and even widening them.

Yishai and John; thank you both!

3

POSSIBILITIES OF THE COLLABORATIVE APPROACH

HARLENE ANDERSON

Harlene Anderson is a founding member of the Houston Galveston Institute, Taos Institute, and AccessSuccess International. She is recognized internationally as being at the leading edge of post-modern collaborative practices as a thinker, consultant, coach, and educator. She embodies her own belief in learning as a life-long process, inviting, encouraging, and challenging people to be inquisitive, creative, authentic, and open to ever-present possibilities for newness in others and in themselves. She is the author of *Conversation, Language, and Possibilities* (1997) and the co-editor (with Diane Gehart) of *Collaborative Therapy: Relationships and Conversations That Make a Difference* (2006).

Nosy Rosy: A Lifelong Learner

Tom told you about his personal journey yesterday. Although many of us here share the same ideas and practices, our journeys are quite different. In terms of my own history, my academic background is in psychology. In 1970 I met Harry Goolishian when I started working at the medical school in Galveston, Texas, and heard about something called "family therapy" that everyone spoke about with a lot of excitement and enthusiasm. My nickname at home when I was young was Nosy Rosy, so I had to find out what this was all about. It was as if I had found something that I didn't know I was looking for. I was fortunate to soon start working with Harry. One of the things that I often hear people say about Harry is that when you were in conversation with him, no matter how short or long the conversation, or no matter how serious or trivial, you always felt as if you were the only person in the room. He really listened to you. He really cared about what you said and you left the conversation having a sense that something had happened that you couldn't quite put your finger on. I think of these kinds of conversations as subtle ones, hardly noticeable in terms of what's happening in the conversation. Lynn Hoffman in her recent book, *Family Therapy: An Intimate History* (2002), referred to Harry's and to my work as "imperceptible." To some it doesn't look like we're doing anything.

Let me tell you a little about where I hang out in Houston. I'm with an organization called the Houston Galveston Institute (HGI) that Harry and I, along with two colleagues, founded in the late 1970s. We're in our 26th year, and the institute has carried on and extended a history of family therapy practice and research that began in Galveston in the 1950s. HGI is a center where we see clients, do research and consultation, and have learning programs. Some of you have visited us. We have a commitment to what we call the "public sector"; to working with clients from child welfare, women's shelters, juvenile justice systems, and schools. We also have an every-other-week seminar for the faculty and the in-house learners. We read literature from both inside and outside the psychotherapy field. We like to think of ourselves as lifelong learners, and important to a lifelong learner is to always have challenges and something new in your life. Although I've been a therapist and a teacher of therapists for many years, recently I've been working with business organizations and their leaders and teams, trying to introduce a collaborative way of organizing and leading. That work affords me to do some things that I really love to do, that I call my volunteer work or donating my time. Later I'm going to tell you about one of these pieces of work.

Basic Assumptions

Language and Knowledge as Relational and Generative

Perhaps I could detour a bit to reiterate and share my perspective of some of the things that Tom was talking about yesterday. Similar to

Tom, I always think of my ideas and work as evolving, that I'm never in any one place too long. I currently refer to my work as a postmodern collaborative approach. I say currently because what I call it and how I think about it shifts. My approach is based on two broad assumptions about language and knowledge. Tom talked about language and the importance of language in our lives, and much like Tom, when I think of language, I think of it as any means that we try to express ourselves or communicate. It can be words, symbols, gestures, eye movements, or the sign pointing to the toilet. Language is the primary vehicle with which we construct our knowledge and develop and convey our meanings about the events and experiences in our lives, about the people we're in relationship with and about ourselves. Knowledge is linguistically constructed; its development is a communal process. Though universal knowledge is ever present and influential, importance is placed on local knowledge that has relevance and usefulness for the participants and their specific, immediate situation. As Tom said, in a certain way, knowledge and language are alive. There's movement, there's creativity to them. I think of knowledge and language as relational and generative, as inherently transforming, or, you might say, transforming is inherent in the communal activity. Though sometimes it seems that things are at a standstill, I think that things are always in motion, always moving. Sometimes they move so slowly that you can't see or feel the motion or the movement.

Collaborative Relationships and Dialogical Conversations

The notion of collaborative relationships and generative conversations flows from this perspective of knowledge and language. The kind of relationship and conversation that I refer to are intertwined and cannot be separated. As Wittgenstein suggested, relationships and conversations go hand in hand. The kind of relationship that you have with another informs and forms the kind of conversations you will be able to have with each other and vice versa.

Collaborative relationship refers to doing something with, rather than to, another person. It refers to a particular way in which we connect, orient ourselves, and interact with another person, inviting the person to mutually engage with us. It refers to joining with another in a shared engagement or a joint activity. These kinds of relationships require genuine trust, openness, and responsiveness to the other.

When people ask, "What are the aspects of a collaborative relationship? What words would you use?" I think in terms of trust and respect as mutual and relational processes between people rather than a basic trait of a person. Each person has a sense of safety with the other. Tom mentioned, and Jaakko writes about, the critical aspect of responding to another person—being responsive to the other person, acknowledging them, and what they say is important. Lastly, one aspect, which people think that I'm not serious about, but when my students ask me what is the most important thing about being in a collaborative relationship as a therapist or as a teacher or researcher, I say, "It's to have good manners." It sounds very simplistic, but if you really think about it, good manners communicate a lot about the way that you think of the other person. I'll talk more about this later.

Likewise, I think of dialogical conversation as a particular way of talking in which participants engage with each other, and with themselves, in which you're involved in a mutual or shared inquiry about the focus of the conversation or the purpose of the meeting. Dialogue involves an inquiry about the issues at hand—jointly examining, questioning, commenting, thinking, and reflecting. It's a process of trying to understand each other's meanings. And in this process, new meanings are generated. I think of all conversations as dialogical, but sometimes in my teaching and writing I use the term *monological* to have something to compare and contrast dialogical with. I think of dialogue as a continuum. Conversations move back and forth along the continuum, sometimes being more, and other times less, dialogical.

For me, what is more important is not whether any one part of a conversation is more or less dialogical, but the wholeness of dialogue or the sense that you are in a dialogue: that you are talking with another person; that each of its members has a sense that they are participating in the dialogue, in the conversation. A sense of participating leads to a sense of belonging and ownership. And, a sense of belonging and ownership invites shared responsibility. Some, who are interested in language-based therapies or language theories, talk about dialogical moments or particular moments in a conversation, as if you can pinpoint them and say, "That's dialogue and that's not."

I don't tend to think that way. I think that if you say something is a dialogical moment, then that's a construction at that point in time. It's a punctuation of your analysis of the conversation. I'm much more interested in clients' descriptions of conversations than therapists'.

Dialogue is a complex activity that cannot be reduced to techniques. As I mentioned regarding the philosophical stance, it is a way of being with, and responding to, an "other" from which dialogical activity naturally develops.

Philosophical Stance

When I think of knowledge and language this way, it invites a worldview that includes the way that I think about the people that I work with and the way I think about myself and my role with them. The worldview is somewhat akin to the movement in psychology in the United States called "positive psychology," though it has a different philosophical and theoretical basis. Positive psychology doesn't focus on deficits or see people as needing to be fixed but focuses rather in terms of possibilities. The descriptions that we have of people create them; that is, we participate in creating the person or the image of the person, in front of us. For me, I think of people as naturally having strengths and resources, and I think that most people want to have happy and live successful and peaceful lives. I think that people have the potential to do what they want to do, to reach their dreams, and that's kind of a gift in my work. In other words, it allows me to see people in a more hopeful way and as having more possibilities. I think this attitude invites and encourages competency and hope in the people with whom I work, and it encourages competency and hope in me as well, which is most important. This is not to say that I ignore or pretend that some people's lives are not as bad, miserable, or painful as they are. Nor is it to say that I look for the positive or try to appeal to others to see things as I do. But I do not let the bad, the misery, or the pain overwhelm me. I am touched by it, take it seriously, and try to learn about it. And in so doing, I engage the other into the mutual inquiry that I mentioned.

In my writings I talk about a philosophical stance, a way of being that flows from the notions of knowledge and language as relational and generative. The stance is a way of being in relationship with, thinking about, and responding with the other person. The philosophical stance is a way of living; it is the manner that one "is" in both professional life and personal life. I don't think in terms of separating one's professional and one's personal life. It's important to be authentic, to have a sense of congruity or consistency in the way you are as a professional and the way you are as a person in your everyday life. I'm often asked, "How can you learn to take this philosophical stance?" My reply is usually, "I'm not sure that you can learn to do this in the sense that it is teachable. The philosophical stance is a belief; if you sincerely believe in and value its assumptions, and if it fits for you deep inside, the belief and value will be expressed in your actions and your words, in your way of being in the world. If that is the case, then you will find yourself spontaneously, genuinely, and naturally acting in particular ways."

I have tagged seven characteristics of therapy based on the assumptions related to the philosophical stance: the notion of collaborative relationships and dialogical conversations. First is (1) the idea of conversational partners. I think of myself and the client as being conversational partners who connect with each other, collaborative with each other, and create with each other. Partners are in-there-together and are more equal to each other than less. Importantly though, we are involved in a particular activity or task that has, and must have, relevance for the client.

(2) The client is the expert. I recently read a journal article in which the author said, "How can Harlene Anderson say that the client is the expert and deny her own expertise?" When I refer to the client as the expert, I'm referring to the client as the expert on his or her life. The client is the expert on his or her story and the contents of the story. The client is the expert on what's important and what's not important to talk about. When I think of the client as the expert, that makes me the learner. The client is my teacher, and I'm learning from them. In my experience, when I'm truly interested in the other person and curious about him or her, my interest and inquisitiveness naturally invites that person into a shared or mutual inquiry or a joint activity. In other words, what might be thought of as starting out as a one-way inquiry or process shifts to a two-way process in which client and therapist

engage in learning and exploring together. I think of it as if a client is handing me a "story ball." Rather than take it from the client, I simply put my hands on it and am curious about what they are showing me. I begin to turn the story ball, looking at it, asking about it. It is as if the client catches my curiosity and begins to wonder with me. As we together turn the ball this way and that, the client takes the lead; I follow the client and pause when and where the client wants to. If I want to pause somewhere or turn the story ball in another direction, I indicate so and ask the client's permission. I follow the client's response. I have no investment that my curiosity should take precedence over that of the client.

"The client is the expert" does not mean that the professional doesn't have any expertise. One way of punctuating it and thinking about it, again, is the client is the expert on content and the therapist is the expert of the particular process—collaborative relationship and dialogical conversation. I'm separating content and process here to make a distinction, though I think they are inseparable.

One of the most provocative things that Harry and I introduced into the literature is (3) the concept of not-knowing. Let me first of all say that not-knowing does not mean that I think I'm ignorant, that I don't know anything, or that I can walk into the professional arena and forget everything I know or think I might know. It does not mean that I pretend to know or use not-knowing in a manipulative way. Not-knowing refers to the way that I think about knowing, the way that I think about what I know or what I think I might know, and the intent with which I offer that knowledge as well as the intent with which I use it, whether that's publicly or privately. By publicly or privately, I mean, in a conversation where I talk out loud, in which I might introduce "knowing" into the conversation through a comment or question, or in an inner conversation in my head. Not-knowing requires rising above what you know or think you know, to meet the other person and join them in a joint activity in which knowledge is created within the ongoing exchanges of dialogue; knowledge that has relevance and usefulness to the participants in the conversation. Also, as Tom mentioned in a slightly different way, we live in a world full of professional knowledge. What I'm most interested in is "local knowledge," the knowledge that we're creating together, again, that has relevance and usefulness.

Next is (4) being public. Michael mentioned and writes about transparency, feminist therapists write about transparency, and so did Carl Rogers, whom I think was the first to introduce the term into the psychotherapy literature. Transparency usually refers to the importance and act of being open, being forthcoming, showing what your thoughts are, and revealing your prejudices or biases. It's a concept that I didn't have a word for, or I should say that I didn't know I was looking for a word for it, until one time I was on an airplane on the way to Norway. Near the end of the long flight, I was finally just able to go to sleep, and the pilot's voice came on the intercom, "Oh you must look outside! The sun is public!" I thought, "How beautiful! The sun is showing itself to us!" I started to use the term or the words *being public*. It refers to the commitment and activity of not operating from hidden or private ideas, thoughts, questions, but rather being open and making them visible. Though I keep in mind that regardless of what I choose to show other persons, what they see or hear and how they interpret it will be uniquely theirs, not mine.

If you're sitting in front of another person and having ideas about that person, or you're wondering something, share that inner conversation with the person. This is not only important in terms of being respectful and ethical, but it's also somewhat of a safeguard against slipping into what you might punctuate as a monological conversation in your own head. It's a safeguard for having an idea, opinion, or judgment about another person that not only might privately direct what you say or do in a particular direction, but also might risk that the therapist's ideas and agenda take up all the room and forget about the client's expertise. Also, as Tom mentioned, he's careful about his timing when he introduces something into a conversation. I always think it's very important to be overly careful, to not only pay attention to the timing when you introduce something, but the manner, the tone, and the attitude in which you introduce it. It's important to offer anything you say as a therapist in a tentative manner or as provisional, and to not offer it with certainty. This includes being able to let go of your offering and having it questioned or challenged.

I want to talk a little about (5) mutual transforming. The kinds of conversations and relationships that I'm talking about are inherently mutually transforming; that is, you cannot have one person, or meaning, in a conversation or relationship change and not the others. Most of us have grown up, so to speak, in a psychotherapy field with the idea that a therapist is an agent of change and that you can change another person. I think each person is changing, that this is a continuous process of being a living human being. I prefer the word *transforming*; one reason is because we've inherited so many words and concepts in the psychotherapy field that come with meanings that don't fit with what I'm trying to convey. Transforming allows me to think of things as continually in motion, continually moving, continually being and becoming.

When you accompany another person on the kind of journey that I'm talking about, in terms of being engaged in a collaborative relationship and a dialogical conversation, it involves (6) uncertainty. The twists and turns that the relationship and the conversation will take and the outcome cannot be predetermined. However, for me, when you trust the other person as an expert on his or her life and its circumstances, and when you trust the local knowledge of the community, whether the community is a family, a classroom, or a company's boardroom, when you trust the natural flow of the conversation, you trust uncertainty.

Another idea that flows from the philosophical stance is that what we meet about in therapy is not thought of as a problem to be fixed, diagnosed, or intervened in; rather, we're simply talking about people and (7) the circumstances of everyday, ordinary life. Problems are not categorized as such, but are everyday, ordinary situations that any one of us could be confronted with. When I say that, I think of the open dialogue at work. The open dialogue teams do not meet psychotic individuals. They meet people in relationships.

I do not think of the philosophical stance as a set of skills or as having techniques. I think that if you hold particular beliefs about the people you work with and yourself, you begin to meet and be with people, you begin to act and respond with them, in the ways that I've been talking about.

Philosophical Stance in Action: Collaboration in Bosnia

Let me tell you a story about some women that my colleague Patricia Blakeney and I met in Bosnia. Patricia received an invitation from a London-based NGO (an international nongovernmental organization) to do some training with the staff of a program they had in Bosnia for women refugees and victims of the war. Patricia, who has worked all over the world in war-torn countries, invited me to join her. This was only my third time working in such a country and my second time in Bosnia. Still being very new to these circumstances, I asked Pat a lot of questions about where we were going and what we were expected to do, but she didn't have a lot of information. She said she knew that the staff had had some previous training, and that it had been called "rape screening and intervention training," for the staff to learn how to screen for women who'd been raped and how to intervene. They had also had training on how to teach or coach victims to testify at the war crime tribunals. She said that she thought that the previous training had been rather traditional in the sense that it was prepackaged and that trainers lectured and taught techniques.

There's a growing body of literature that's very challenging and critical of Western psychological intervention models in international work where people have been victims of war and other kinds of tragedies. There's a call for a more community-based and participatory approach that uses the expertise of the individual, the family, and the community members and that pays attention to the larger cultural and institutional context, especially the local people's, *and* the local helpers' definitions of their problems and needs and the kind of help they want. This represents a move away from professionals coming in and training local helpers that they view as less professional, because many of the helpers are people who have also been victims and have lived in the same circumstances as those they are trying to help.

When I asked Pat why she wanted me to come with her on this particular occasion, she, in her very casual way and with her teasing smile, said, "I think you can adjust to any situation." I wasn't quite sure what that meant in terms of what I was going to get myself into. After a long plane ride and a seemingly longer bumpy car ride from Sarajevo to Tuzla, although we were tired, we did not turn down the invitation from the acting director to have dinner with her and the woman whose home we'd live in. For us, joining them was important for several reasons: We could tell that they had planned on our joining them, so we didn't want to inconvenience or disappoint them; we would learn something about what the acting director and the staff expected of us; and the acting director would be a bridge between us and the staff that we would meet the next morning. What we learned over a hearty home-cooked dinner (yes, they were expecting us to accept their invitation) was that although the London-based office had invited us to do what they called "psychosocial training," the acting director said that she and the staff wanted us to focus on the problems of violence, particularly adolescent and criminal violence. We also learned that historically the program had had an English director, but they had not had a director for almost a year. Although the acting director and the staff felt like a loose ship at sea and wanted a director, there was some apprehension. We learned that the previous director came from a very psychodynamic orientation, stayed very separate from the staff, and never tried to speak or learn Bosnian. Based on other things that we learned about the director, it seemed that she lived her theoretical prejudice, that is, her idea of the importance of maintaining boundaries. The acting director also told us that she and the staff were concerned about future funding, because many of the NGOs who had been providing money for psychosocial services to help rebuild the country had either already pulled out or had announced plans to do so. We learned later how "real" this fear was, since the staff had not been paid in 3 months because of the funding problems.

Early the next morning the program van, crammed with staff members, arrived to pick us up and we squeezed in. This seemed to be a morning ritual and luxury, staff getting a ride to the center. When we arrived at the center, some of the staff was already making coffee, which seemed to be another morning ritual in which each member had her role. They offered Pat and me coffee, and then all of them went outside of the building onto the small entry landing to have their coffee and a smoke. Pat and I decided we would join them even though the weather was dreary, freezing cold, and raining. We thought we would try to get to know them a little bit. But we didn't speak Bosnian and only a few of them spoke some English words, so we communicated through gestures. They were friendly, but not overly so. The staff were all women.

Almost on the dot at 8:15, all of the women walked back into the building to an upstairs room, so Pat and I followed them. This was the room where we were going to have our consultation/training. The tables were arranged in a rectangle. The staff seated themselves around the table and we took the last two seats, which happened to be the two seats next to whom we learned was the volunteer translator. All of us kept our coats on because it was so cold in the building. There were 17 women around the table: 14 of them were staff members and 3 of them were guests. One guest was a teacher from a French organization, one was a social worker from a Swiss organization, and the third was the translator, who was a college graduate in some area of literature. Pat and I then more formally introduced ourselves and told them how pleased we were to be there, which we were.

Connecting and Responding

We asked them, "Could we go around the table and have each person say your name, your role, something about your work at the center, and anything else that you, at this time, want us to know about you." As the introductions began, I took a piece of paper, because this was a very poor organization and there were no writing tablets or blackboards, and I went around the table and as each woman introduced herself, I tried to write her name on the paper. I had to ask them to help me with the pronunciations and spellings. Pat and I then tried to pronounce the names; Pat was much better at it than I was.

I'm walking you through these steps to help you have a sense of my work and how I begin to meet and greet people and how this sets the tone for the kinds of relationships and conversations that I talked about earlier. I think of myself as a momentary guest in my clients' lives while at the same time I am their host. With my students, we talk about being a "good" guest and host and what that entails and how the guest–host metaphor links to the philosophical stance.

In terms of being public and the client being the expert, when Pat and I introduced ourselves to them, we shared what the London office had requested for the training and the conversation that we had had with the acting director the night before about what she said that she and the staff wanted the training to focus on. We said, "However, we would like to learn more about your specific, your more individual agendas." We asked them questions such as, "How would you like to use this time?" "What would you like to accomplish?" and "Are there questions about your work you would like to discuss?" We really wanted to learn from them why they were there (other than they had been told to be there) and what they wanted or hoped we could offer or help with. I don't think in terms of consensus, that we have a consensus agenda or that we're going to collapse all of the interests in two or three main topics. I want to know as much as possible about each person's beginning ideas and expectations, whether they're similar or different. I want to, what I call, keep those differences, all those unique voices, in the air. Just as I wrote their names, I also wrote their questions and agenda items. It's a way of acknowledging the other persons and responding to them. However, if they said they wanted to talk about adolescent violence toward younger members in the family, I didn't just write those words on my paper and then move on to the next person. I tried to learn more about their words, more about what they wanted to talk about, more what they wanted to "know" or help with. Connecting and responding with the other person is a continuing process. You begin to create an environment in which you're doing something with the other rather than doing something to or for them, and you continually try to foster the environment.

Local Knowledge

We learned that the staff had varied experiences and educational levels. Three of them were refugees who had lost their homes and were forced to move and start over. We learned that all of the staff had learned to do their work "by doing," by improvising and supporting each other as they worked with their clients, the women victims of the war. We also learned that most of the staff's work was done in the field, in the areas where their clients lived. They worked in teams of two, three or four, and they went to approximately 17 settlement centers—like refugee centers that are built to house people who have been displaced. They also went to areas of the city where the refugees or displaced persons had taken over the vacant homes of local citizens who had fled the war. At the time that we were there, there was a lot of political and social upheaval between these two groups of people, those coming back to reclaim their homes and the people living in them who refused to leave.

We also learned that the deserted homes that had been occupied by the refugees had multiple families and people living in them, with usually one family or several persons living in one or two rooms. Though several people lived under the same roof, they were fairly isolated and tended not to leave their homes. The staff told us that when they went to meet with the women in their homes, the men would go to the other room, if there was one, or they'd go outside. They had little or no interaction with the men or the older male children. Many of the women they worked with either lived alone or with other female family members, because the men in their families—the husband, the father, and the male children—had been killed.

Later in the week Pat and I went out in the field with the staff and met some of the women and families. The women we met were welcoming and gracious, always offering coffee. It was obvious that they really liked the staff. Their homes or their rooms were rather barren, with very little furniture, a few kitchen utensils, a few knick-knacks, and a photo or two, usually of a dead loved one. There was little food. There were no jobs. There were no utilities. They burned small logs in a cooking stove that also served for heat.

One of the other things that they do in their work is to offer their services at what's called the Commemorative Center. Pat and I were privileged to accompany them on a trip to the center. We didn't quite know where we were going, but it ended up being one of the most powerful experiences in my life. The Commemorative Center is where, when they dug up the mass graves, they brought the remains of the bodies and the personal belongings. It had a large covered area, where they would put the possessions in little piles with a number. It might be a muddy pair of shoes, a torn piece of clothing; it might be a wallet or a comb. Family members would come and walk around and look at the little piles of possessions and see if they could identify any of the items as belonging to a lost loved one, a man or a boy in their family. If the family member(s) recognized or thought that something belonged to a missing relative, they were taken over to the side and shown photographs of the body. If they recognized the body or felt that the person was a member of their family, they went to a building where there was DNA testing. They would draw blood to do a DNA match. Although this was an . . . it's hard to find a word for it— "extremely interesting experience" does not capture it, is not respectful enough. The air was heavy and solemn though some people were crying, some wailing. There was a sense of lost people. It was a very emotional experience and a very awkward feeling to be intruding on such intimate and moving moments, to be present while trying not to be present. We were alongside the workers as they were talking with the family members, but trying not to be intrusive or disrespectful, especially when it was so obvious that Pat and I were strangers. We remained silent, not being spoken to or speaking with anyone except with eyes. But, back to the earlier part of the story.

Collaborative Partnership in Action

The staff shared their agenda items with us, and a long list of questions and requests for information emerged. As the staff talked, Pat and I were struck by the mood and the emotions in the room. The staff frequently used the word *hopeless* or *helpless:* "We feel hopeless, we feel helpless." These two words caught our attention, so Pat and I talked out loud with each other, we reflected with each other in front of them about how we were struck by these words and the sense of the hopelessness and helplessness that filled the room. We said that it felt like they were buried, motionless, under a mountain of refugee problems. We asked them, "Is this an issue you'd like to talk about more?" They all either said or shook their heads "yes." Though Pat and I could have continued with the agenda and moved on, finding ways to talk about the topics they wanted to talk about, we chose to respond to this feeling in the room because it seemed to be what they were expressing the most and were most occupied by. We asked them to form three conversational clusters and asked each of the three guests—the two visiting workers and the translator—to divide among the clusters. We asked them to talk with each other about their feelings of hopeless and helpless. We posed some questions, such as "What does hopeless and helpless look like?" What do they feel like?" "What metaphors come to mind?" "What colors would you paint these words?" They talked intensely though solemnly with each. We then invited them to come back and re-form as the larger group and for each cluster to share some of their conversation with the rest of us.

Let me say it's important that if they had signaled in any way to us that they didn't want to talk about hopeless and helpless, we would have proceeded with what they wanted to talk about. It was not important to us that they talk about hopeless and helpless; we didn't have an agenda for that. We were trying to be responsive to what we thought they were signaling to us. One might argue that because Pat and I were in positions of power or authority, they might have passively submitted to what they thought we wanted them to do, or what they thought they should do. I have found that when you give room to the other's voice and are respectful of it, and that if you proceed with caution, people begin to feel trusting and safe. I find that they do express themselves and that they will express disagreement or correct you on something that they think is incorrect.

Let me tell you some of their words, some of the things that they said. They said, "Gray and dark colors." "We really cannot help." "We feel the same as a baby who cries, and no one can help because they don't know what the problem is." One said, "We're angry at ourselves, we're not guilty, we didn't cause the problem, but we're angry at the government and the institutions for not supporting us." They said, "Sometimes we are not able to help because we have similar problems." You often hear this latter comment in this kind of work: The staff and the workers experience the same problems as the people they try to help. Others said, "It's like we can't build a tunnel to get out." "It's like being in a desert desperately searching for water." "It's really sad." "We wish we could just disappear."

You can imagine the grave tone and the growing heaviness in the room as each cluster of women shared their words with the others. As they were talking, just as when they were sharing their agenda items, Pat and I were responding to them, making comments and asking questions, to try to understand and learn more about their experiences and their meanings. After they had finished and after a long pause,

Pat and I turned and talked with each other about how, in our bodies, we could feel the sense of helplessness and hopelessness.

We had the sense from the little we knew about them and their work that they were very dedicated to the women they worked with and that they persevered to help them in spite of the overwhelming challenges they faced. But still, they were not sure that they were or could be helpful. We asked each other, "What if there was some small possibility that they could 'help' and that they could regain some 'hope'?" We also said, "This would make a big difference in the way that we continued this consultation and training." It would influence the kinds of conversations that you can have about violence. That is, it is one thing to think about how to approach something when you feel you can't help and there's no hope, versus approaching something when you feel that maybe you can help and maybe you can hope. We asked them if they would be willing to talk about the word *hope*. We were not trying to get them to see hope; we were not trying to move them in that direction. We were simply trying to learn more about what they were referring to and to find some ways to talk about something that seemed very difficult and which they hadn't been able to talk about or, in their opinions, deal with successfully.

As Pat and I continued to talk with each other, we said, "What if we can do this in an imaginative or creative way?" An idea emerged as we talked. We suggested to them that they go back to the earlier conversational clusters, and we would like for each cluster to come up with a Bosnian word that signaled, signified, or meant hope. We asked them to then to write that word vertically on a piece of paper. Then for each letter in the word, see if they could expand or clarify or broaden the definition or the meaning of the word *hope*. It was amazing; as they moved into their clusters, the atmosphere in the room began to shift. They became engaged with each other; they were talking rapidly, with lots of animation. You could see the energy growing. My colleague Pat turned to me and said, "Why don't we do this also?" We chose the word *chocolate*. (We had brought chocolates from the duty-free shop to share with the staff at the end of the training.)

Everything came up with circles around money and vacations. One group had written the word *nagragda*, which means salary. They said, "We need money, we need a car or plane, to go on a holiday on the

Adriatic Sea and we need God to help us, Amen." All of the groups wanted to go to the sea, which is interesting, because I just read a paper by one of our colleagues in Israel, who does training with a staff in a somewhat similar situation. She wrote that when she and her colleagues arrived to do the training, the staff didn't want it. They had had enough of training, and they didn't want someone to teach them techniques on how to deal with stress. They wanted to share their stories about their work and talk about the pain and being burned out by work. The influence of their work on them as human beings was similar to what the Tuzla staff was expressing. Pat and I silently listened to them as they talked with each other. When they came back as the larger group, interestingly, each cluster presented what they had come up with in little poems and songs. They were so touching and creative. As we had a general discussion, Pat and I tried to pull out what we called "discussion questions," questions that had surfaced from the larger conversation about the cluster conversations. In other words, we were trying to capture what they were saying in their words. This conversation paused, as it was time for a lunch break. The staff left for lunch, talking lively with each other.

I always want to try to understand the other person, and to do that I must respond to them; I must try to check out to see if what I think I've heard is what they wanted me to hear. In so doing, I can't simply just say their words back to them that they said to me. If I simply do that, then neither of us would know whether I've heard or not. You have to respond to the other with what you think they said, using different words. You have to have something to compare and contrast it with. I think, as Tom was referring to, you want to stay close to their original language. Again, I want to make sure that I am hearing or understanding as best I can what it is they want me to hear or understand. I'm not trying to purposely introduce new ideas, words, or meanings into the conversation by using different words, although, of course, some words may remain in the conversation. [Based on the conference schedule, it was time for Harlene to pause her presentation and for others to reflect and pose questions.]

Discussion

Harlene: Now you can pose your reflections, questions, or opinions, and I will listen and offer my reflections on your reflections. So, gentlemen...?

Michael: Does that include me?

Harlene: That includes you, Michael, most definitely.

Tom: Come on, Michael.

Michael: Well, I was drawn to many, many aspects of this presentation and I guess one of the things that really struck a powerful chord for me was what Harlene was saying about how she joined with this group and invited them to render things like helplessness or hopelessness more tangible. By inviting these women to speak about what helpless or hopeless would look like, what color they would be, or what metaphors would come to their mind, how does it feel... I was drawn to that, because helpless and hopeless can be so overwhelming, so pervasive that to render it tangible, I'm sure opens up some space in engaging with other sentiments of life. So I was quite drawn to that.

Jaakko: I was also thinking that it's so easy to follow the plan that we make after collecting all those points that they have said. Pat and Harlene were so sensitive to change the plan.

Jaakko: Tom, do you have ideas?

Tom: I wonder what you were thinking when she said, "There's no separation between professional and personal life." What were you thinking when she said that?

Michael: I was thinking two things about that. For me, there are distinct differences between a therapeutic relationship and the relationships of my personal life. The other thing I was thinking about was the sentiment "not to split the professional and the personal"—the importance of being aware of what touches us in professional conversations. Therapeutic conversations can touch people's lives, but the life of the therapist is also changed for this. This is not a one-way process. Like Harlene said, "It's a two-way process." My life is touched by my work, and I know that this affects my life, my relationships with other people, in a multiplicity of ways; for example, this can open up possibilities for conversation with friends and family I might not have otherwise had, or contribute to new understandings of my own history. I think it's important that I acknowledge this to the people who are consulting me. Tom, what were you thinking?

Tom: Well, actually I thought I would have liked very much for Harlene to say something more. I would like you to say more. This is crucial. One other big point was being public, and she said, "not operating from private hidden ideas" but rather "opening up and making them more visible." It comes to that other sentence of private and personal. I wonder what is a hidden idea?

Jaakko: I don't have an answer for that, I'm thinking of the first question: Is there a difference between private and professional life? I have a tendency to think about it the same way as Harlene said because there's one life. I have one life that I'm living, but in many voices. These voices are switched on, depending on which kind of context, which kind of situation, relations, people, in which surroundings we are living. I very much hope that the things I do follow the same kind of moral and ethical values that I think are important. Of course I act differently in a professional situation than with my friends and so on, but still thinking that's my life.

Michael: I was thinking about what Harlene was saying about good manners. I like this idea very much. It's also another example of refusing to conceive of a professional world that's separate from the personal world. I was thinking about hospitality and what a difference it makes when we sit down with people, and our conversations are in part shaped by practices of hospitality.

Tom: I still hope Harlene will say more about not separating professional and private life and about hidden ideas. When she spoke, she made a comment of coming into the room, and she mentioned how the table was arranged. If she has an idea about that arrangement, should it be hidden or should it be spoken? It's an interesting expression, "hidden ideas."

Should all of our prejudices be spoken, or should we keep them held back? That would be interesting to hear. Is it possible to not have a hidden idea? Where do we hide it? Also I like the words *good manners* very much. She also spoke of responsiveness, openness, and the two words *trust* and *respect*. Where do we find trust and respect? Where are they?

Jaakko: Should we give Harlene the opportunity to comment?

Who's the Host and Who's the Guest?

Harlene: Sure, personal and professional. I want to expand on that a little bit. I don't think I can be one person in the therapy room or in the classroom and another person or a third person in my home with my family or at a restaurant with friends. The values I carry with me, the way I handle myself, my style, and so on, there's a congruency in that. Sometimes people have the idea when you go into the therapy room, you have to totally change: You have a white coat and a list of questions, you behave a certain way called "professional," you maintain boundaries, and you don't self-disclose. I think that the parts of us that we show or that are drawn out, or the voice or voices we use, are very much context and relationship dependent. I do think that the therapy room is a particular context with a particular agenda and expectations, and I would want to match some of those and maybe not match some of them. We are multiple selves. We fit in or adapt to a given context and relationship; parts of us come forth in certain situations and not others. We carry the same values everywhere we go, the same biases, the same prejudices, and the same assumptions. There is congruency.

So yes, if I'm sitting in a therapy room with a client, much like you said, Michael, I think this is not a restaurant conversation. There are differences in these kinds of conversations, particularly their agenda. But who I am is pretty much the same. With the students I have in the university, I always challenge some of the inherited traditions or theoretical ideas that they bring with them—like boundaries

of self-disclosure. Some of my strong ideas about this have
come from my years of interviewing clients about their experiences of successful therapy, as well as what they said about
therapists whom they thought were helpful. I don't remember exactly, but the therapist's presence or lack of it came up
in Tom's presentation in the after-interview. Clients often
felt and expressed it with words such as, "I felt like I was
sitting in there naked and the therapist knew everything
about me, but I didn't know anything about him or her and
if I asked them, they interpreted that in some way." It's like
we're human beings, and the therapist is as much a human
being in the relationship as is the client.

If you're in a relationship, any kind of relationship, you
are another human being whether the relationship takes
place in a therapy room, a consultation room, a classroom,
or a prison. That's also part of what I think about in terms
of personal and professional. I also suggest to the students,
when they work with me, that we will be unlearning a lot
of what we learned in graduate school. Like you said about
hospitality, I often use the guest–host metaphor, and I say to
my students, "Think as if you are the host and they are your
guest, while at the same time they're the host and you're the
guest; you're the guest in their life." "Forget about the questions you're supposed to ask, or how you're supposed to sit
and look as a therapist." How can you just sit down and talk
with a person like you would do with anyone else that you
meet? I have strong ideas about that, so I resonate with your
idea about hospitality.

Tom: When you spoke, you used the phrase "no separation of personal
and professional life." What I think I'd like to do is to make
a clear division between professional and personal. I say to
myself, "This is not my time when we are here in this room,
it's their time. I have my time another time." That's one thing
I say. The other is that there are a lot of things going on, as I'm
sure also happens when you're talking. That's where the hard
work is going on. Many ideas emerge during your talk. If I
were to launch one of the ideas, then I ask the other person,

pointing back to our conversation, "When you said this or that, some thoughts came to me. Would you be interested to hear them?" I always ask that. Until now everybody has said, "Yes, I want to hear them." It's very important, because they are their words, and there is a chance to enlarge or widen the words with some of your thoughts. If there's a "No, I'm not interested," it will disappear. I have a lot of hidden thoughts, which I don't speak. Harlene has a lot of thoughts going on; she's a hard inner talker and you do a lot of work with the inner talk, which remains as inner talk. I do not know, but that's what I assume.

We had an interesting talk in Sweden where the team sat in the after-talk. There was so much noise that we were afraid in the team. I said, "In hindsight, was it possible to talk about your fear with the family?" They said, "No, I'm not sure." The mother said, "I'm so glad you didn't speak of your fear, because we were so fearful—we were fearful enough." I think there are many things we should not say.

Harlene: I totally agree with you that therapy time is the client's time. It's not my time. In agreeing with that, I think that is different from what I'm talking about in terms of the professional and the personal. I'm talking more about the way of being, the way I am in the world. I'm pretty much the same in different contexts and relationships, although I mentioned earlier some contexts and relationships might draw one aspect of me more forward than another; I want to match the context and relationship as best I can. I totally agree that therapy time is for the client.

When you said something about "Can anything be hidden?" I started thinking about that. When you're thinking about something, unless it can be made to fade away or be overridden by other aspects of the conversation, you might communicate it in ways that you don't realize—by your attitude or your tone, or through your eyes. If you feel disgust for a person, for example, that might come through your eyes although you try to hide it. Maybe there is nothing that is really hidden. What I'm really talking about in terms of the hidden or private is that if you have an idea or a set of ideas rolling around in your head that's affecting how you hear, see, and respond to the other person, it's influencing your comments and questions. There is the risk of slipping into more of the monologic mode. There is also the risk of going down a narrow path and perhaps more the path that the therapist wants to follow or more the story that the therapist wants to hear rather than the path that the client wants to take or the story that the client wants to tell.

When I start to talk to someone, I usually take a broader sweep or a scanning, never staying in any one area for too long for risk of having too much influence on the direction of conversation. "Can we talk about this? Then, about this? We might come back to this." Which direction does the client want to take? Where does the client want to pause? I talk about the notion of being public with the learners at the institute and the university where I teach because I find it's easy for beginning therapists to have, what I call, some pretty negative judgments or cultural biases about people. For instance, if you're talking with a mother and you're thinking, "This is an overprotective mother," then how does that description influence how *you* hear what she says and what *you're* trying to accomplish? I try to help people be able to deal with those kinds of thoughts.

When you find yourself a prisoner of an idea or a thought, there are many ways to handle it. You can handle it through your inner talk. You can handle it through saying it out loud in some way and, again, paying careful attention to your timing and the words you choose. You can do a variety of other things, and I think it would be different for each of us.

Tom: Very clarifying for me.

Jaakko: This is an interesting point you are making. I, of course, agree with the idea that being public does not mean that we reveal all hidden thoughts or secrets. I think the idea that some thoughts are hidden or public is problematic in itself because they are in a movement all the time. For me, the idea is to think in meetings, "How we can proceed in generating more dialogue?" Of course the thing that is taking place within my inner dialogue, all the negative feelings or anger or irritation with something that is said, it's not a dialogue only to put those in the open. The selection happens in some way, as Michael would perhaps say, resonating with the things that are taking place in the conversation. I think it's interesting.

Tom: The concept of open dialogue, if one takes it too literally, could also be misunderstood.

Jaakko: Yeah, definitely. For instance, there are people who have come to a presentation and listen to that and say, "I will absolutely not come to a meeting where I will publicly speak of my individual psychotherapy relation with the patient." There are a lot of possibilities to misunderstand it.

Michael: I think that it's not just a matter of what thoughts we express or what experiences we express. It's also the responsibility we take for the shape that we give to that expression. I don't think it's a question about whether we speak about what's resonating with us or not, but it's about the shape we give to that expression. We are responsible for the consequences of what we do or say.

I work a lot with what Tom might describe as reflecting teams. The word I use is *outsider witnesses*. There are skills for us to be developing in our work with people, whether we are working as therapists or reflecting team members. Outsider witnesses go through a range of experiences in response to listening to powerful stories of life, and sometimes they hear things that touch on painful experiences of their own history. The question is not whether or not they're public about something that's so visible anyway, but it's a question about how they give expression to these painful experiences. An outsider witness might say, "I witnessed this reunion between mother and daughter, and I found this powerful. It was also painful for me, because I didn't have a connection like this with my own mother." But to say this is not enough. It's important for the outsider witness to go beyond this and to also speak about what this pain is a reflection of in terms of what the outsider witness is valuing.

I was thinking about Tom's presentation of this man who was restless. On the other side of this restlessness was a searching. This man's restlessness was in relation to something. This has me thinking about Jacques Derrida's notions about the absent but implicit. There's always something absent but implicit in everyone's expression. For example, what was absent but implicit in this expression of pain on behalf of the outsider witness is a longing for a specific relationship with her own mother, which she'd held on to all these years. The outsider witness also has the opportunity to go beyond this: "This is the first time I've really publicly acknowledged that longing in this way, in this conversation." It's not just about what people express. It's about the responsibility they take for the shape they give to this expression.

For the mother and daughter to think that the outsider witness was left in pain on account of their reunion can be problematic. For them to be aware that ripples of their story touched the outsider witness in ways that made it possible for them for the first time to publicly acknowledge something that has been precious to them over all these years, this is something else again. It has a lot to do with the skills that we make it our business to develop so we can express what we are experiencing in ways that are in harmony with our ethical responsibility to families.

Ways of Bending Back

Jaakko: You are talking about outsider witnessing. Do you mean people who are sitting in some other place, in the room, or...?

Michael: They are usually in the same place, but I wasn't meaning to just focus on the responses of the outsider witnesses. It's the same for us as therapists. We have a range of experiences of our work, and I don't think it's a matter of do we obscure this or not. It's about the care that we take in the ways that we give expression to them. I see a lot of this in

Tom's work and Harlene's work. There is a lot of care taken in your expressions.

Jaakko: There is a difference if we are sitting in the same circle or if the ones who are reflecting are sitting in a different position. I have a lot of consultation situations when there is a 20-person team present. Two or three can be sitting with the family in the circle, and the others are around them. The experience, although we are sitting in the same room, becomes different among us sitting inside the circle. I do not have any need to have guiding rules to the comments. I can totally trust what they are speaking, but I have become more and more cautious with the comments outside. Nowadays I have rules for how I want them to speak. They can be listening to the discussion, but only listening as if they are being the mother or as the father or as the therapist, and so on. I really think from a dialogical point of view there are lots of differences if we are sitting bodily connected in the same circle, or if we give our reflection through a position looking from outside, although sitting in the same room.

Tom: Some small points about so-called reflecting talks! I would prefer the words *reflecting teams* be taken away. There are so many different reflecting talks. I used to say to those I have spoken with, "There have been some people listening to us; would you be interested to hear their thoughts?" If they say, "Yes," I say, "Please do what feels more comfortable for you, either listen to them, or maybe you will notice that your mind is going to other places; just let that happen. Or if you want to rest and do something else . . ." Then I speak to the other people and say, "I shall not instruct you, but if you are able to keep your talk between yourselves, which means not talking to the family or looking at them, I think it will be better. That lets them have a chance between listening and letting the mind go. The second you look at a person when you speak, they start to work on the answers to it." That is very important for me, letting the others have a chance not to listen.

Harlene: Well, I do not give reflectors instructions. I prefer that people say what they prefer to say.

Tom: Also let them speak to the person?

Harlene: Well, I don't set rules about that. I might ask them to talk among themselves though I find often that's difficult for people to do. I don't want to interfere with what they will say or how they express themselves, but I do agree that this requires care. I do agree that once a reflector starts speaking to, and looking at, the person who's listening, that this interrupts the speaking and listening positions. The people speaking then don't have the time to fully finish their thoughts, and the people listening can't really be in a listening mode because they're now engaging and responding with the reflectors. I think that if you're in your own conversational circle and you're having a conversation among yourselves and you're not directly engaging the other person, the other person is better able to attend and listen. Both speaking and listening require uninterrupted space and time.

The other thing that I find is that it's totally unpredictable, at least in my work, what a client will choose to be drawn by, what will really resonate with the listener. In terms of the content... there are many ways to express an idea, a question, a description, and so forth. There are ways to say it that can be received as very insulting or very judgmental. There are also ways to say it in which what is expressed is not off-putting. I do not suggest that the intent of the reflection should be agreement, but that the reflection and the manner in which it is offered does not negatively interfere with relationship or the conversation.

Michael: I would be very interested to have a further conversation about the way you both think about the audience's participation. What word do you use for the audience people now? They're not reflecting... What are they now? Do you have a word?

Tom: Yes, I use the word *reflect*. *Reflect* means to "bend back," "reflect." What I call them... some people in the room.

Michael: I structure the re-tellings quite strongly. Very often in unstructured situations the outsider witness will respond with the superlative: "This person's amazing." I'll ask, "What did you hear that caught your attention? What were the words? What was the sentiment that you were drawn to?" What's necessary is a rich description of the expression that the outsider witness was drawn to. Then I'm likely to ask, "What mental pictures came to your mind, or what metaphors came to your mind at this time? How did this affect your image of these people's lives and identities?" Once again, I'm not asking for advice or opinion. I really want to know what the expressions evoked in the mind of the outsider witness.

The third thing I want to know is about the resonances of the outsider witness. It's not by chance that a person is drawn to some expression. Their interest is not academic; it's personal. It's not an armchair interest; it's personal interest. I want to know what the expressions touched on for the outsider witness.

The fourth thing I want to know is where it transported the outsider witness to, where it took them. The outsider witnesses have been attentive to a powerful drama of life. They've been taken to a place in their thoughts and perceptions that they wouldn't otherwise be taken to. I structure re-tellings through my questions, and I'd be interested in having more conversation with you about this. How do you deal with the judgments that people make when they are reflecting on the lives of others?

Tom: In our training program, when I work with a group, after we've heard people telling something, I usually encourage them to first summarize what they've heard. Then maybe I would ask, "What did you feel was most important for the person to say?" That in itself is very important; that is the witnessing part.

Michael: That is structuring.

Tom: That is connected to a well-known saying by Wittgenstein. In one of his books, he says, "Away with all theories. We must stop all explanations, and descriptions must come in their place." This is saying what we heard is a description.

Michael: That actually limits people's possibilities to create hypotheses or theorize about people's lives, and that's important.

Tom: And maybe in training, I could say, "What of that you heard moved you the most?"

Harlene: I think everything has a structure. Some things are more structured and some things are less structured. I want to come back to that. One of the things I think about with Tom saying, "I don't talk about the reflecting team anymore," is that I don't either and I encourage people not to because of what's happened with it. It's become a technique rather than thinking of it as a concept that can be operationalized in many ways. What I hear is that it's a concept that the three or four of us would operationalize in different ways. I don't do it the same way every time if I ask for reflections. It depends on the conversation and context; it can take a variety of shapes and forms.

Jaakko: One part of the structuring of the situation is the conversation itself. In the conversation, those who are active are formulating the questions and focusing on different things instead of some other things, and those listening to the conversation are also structured in their thoughts because, in their thoughts, they are following what is discussed and not the things that are not discussed. I don't give a structure as challenging their comments in any way, but my structure for the comments afterward would be like, "I would very much like you not to speak to the clients, because I want them to have the choice to listen or not, and they perhaps will have more space for their thoughts. You can speak to each other, or you can speak to me."

Harlene: Anything left over from reflections that I haven't responded to?

Trust—A Relational Way of Being or Practice

Tom: (To Harlene) Where do you find trust? Where is it?

Harlene: I think trust is between people; it's an interactive aspect of life. I don't think of it as an internal characteristic, but as something that develops in a relationship; it has to be mutual. I don't think you can make someone trust you or talk someone into trusting you. You have to act and behave and talk in ways that are trustful.

Tom: I like this neither/nor; it's neither that nor that, but it's here. I cannot see it, but it's here. Pärt (an Estonian composer) said that the angels are all over but we don't see them, and he says air is full of music, but very many don't hear it. But I hear it, and I put it down on paper.

Michael: I hear two concepts of trust here. One is that it's something that is a metaphysical development. But I also hear you talking about a relationship practice. You talk and act in trusting ways, so you guide the development of the relationship with the concept of trust. You're engaging in a practice, and this practice has been developed ahead of a relationship that you have with someone consulting you.

Harlene: That's a vocabulary that you use that I don't, a vocabulary of practices.

Michael: I don't want to impose this.

Harlene: No, I know, I'm just making a distinction. I think of it more as a way of being, when you think of it as practices. We might be talking about the same thing, but we're using different words.

Michael: There's an actuality to it, isn't there? A way of speaking, a tone of voice . . .

Harlene: There is a way of speaking, tone of voice, manner, and the attitude that you convey . . .

Michael: Timing?

Harlene: Timing, and whether you're careful or careless. All of those, plus other things, combine to signal to another person that there's some trust. Timing, but also time; it takes time, familiarity, for trust to develop between people.

Michael: Would *skill* be a word that you relate to? Would you say that you have some skills?

Harlene: It's not a word that I relate to. The reason I have a lot of difficulty with that word is that it's one of those words that we've inherited. It's a skill, it's a technique, something that you learn to do and you apply it across these kinds of situations or characteristics in people or problems. I'm trying, in my own work in helping people to learn to be therapists, to move them away from thinking that there's a skill recipe or set of methods that we learn and apply time after time. I'm not suggesting that that's what you're suggesting, but I become very cautious when there are skills or techniques.

Tom: Can I ask Jaakko a question?

Harlene: Yes.

Tom: What would Mikhail Bakhtin say about trust? He's a Bakhtin star.

Jaakko: Yes, I'm in love with him although he doesn't know it. Perhaps he'd be pointing to the idea that if people are heard, that's the beginning of trust. Actually, I started to think of a consultation that happened in a South European city. We met a family, it was a consultation situation, and I was sitting in the circle with the psychiatrist, the therapist, and the family, including the mother, father, and a son of 25 years of age. The family therapists were around us, about 20 of them. Before starting the conversation, I asked them, "Would it be okay if I gave a task for the people sitting around?" My proposal was that they'd be divided so that some of them only listen to how it feels to be the mother, some others the father, and so on. Then I asked, "Who would be the best to start?" The father said immediately, "It's the mother." Once she started to speak, she was speaking for 17 minutes. It was in an extremely negative manner about her son, who is all wrong, is not going to the therapy, is not taking care of his life, and so on and so on. I have to say that I had to bite my tongue to not go and interrupt, but I thought that this seems to be so difficult that the only way for her to go further was if she gets a feeling that she is heard in this conversation. It continued 17 minutes and after that, I took a break to wait if she really was finished; I waited about 20 to 30 seconds.

Then I asked the father. After I had had some words with him, the mother said, very offended, "I am always interrupted." What happened afterward was when these family

therapists listening to the mother gave such beautiful comments on her situation, she could not avoid feeling that they
really understood her. I suppose it was one of the first times
in this difficult history of her son's problems that she really
became heard. It was like a cloud of understanding came
into the room, and it was a moving experience. A change
happened at that time, and I think that was the start of
trust. If you become heard, that's the main point.

Harlene: I also think that in order for there to be room for me, there
first has to be room for you.

Tom: Did you hear Bakhtin's voice in that talk?

Jaakko: Yeah, perhaps a lot of that. Bakhtin is also saying that for
a human being, there is nothing as terrible as a lack of
response. That's good advice. It's very concrete advice for
me. I know that there is nothing as terrible for the people
sitting with me, if I don't answer them.

Michael: Anyway, I was thinking about how strongly I feel linked
to that in externalizing practices. I see a similarity here.
Something like helplessness or hopelessness is externalized and made more tangible. This is one of the chords that
was really struck for me. I had a strong resonance, a strong
appreciation for how you opened the space for that woman
to speak of other things as well.

Harlene: I like the idea of dialogical processes and conversations. I'm
also interested in the idea of staying close to people's language, to their words. However, how do you handle the situation or respond when people want you to take the expert
position, when they seem to push you to come up with an
idea, and may disengage with you, if you don't respond to
their stated objective? Well, when you have a client that says,
"Tell me what to do," or "What advice do you have?" I think,
as we were talking a moment ago, it is extremely important
to respond and not ignore their question or request. I also
think it's important to not interpret their question or their
request. If someone says, "What would you do if you were
in this situation?" or "What do you think I should do?" I
will respond to that. My response, however, will be based in

the context and relationship of that local conversation. So, there would be a variety of responses that I could possibly imagine. It might be, "Right now, I don't have any ideas about what you should do or what I would do if I were in your situation. However, when I have an idea, or if I have an idea, I will share that with you." Or I might say, "As a matter of fact, as we've been talking, two or three things have occurred to me." Or I might say, "I was talking with another mother once and she had a similar dilemma, and I can share with you what we came up with if you would like to hear that. I'm not sure if it will fit or not." I also would want to pose several ideas or options in my response so as to not give the impression that I have the best one for them to take. But, here are some things we can consider, we can talk about. Whatever my response might be, I want to think of it as an "offering into" the conversation, as what I call "more food for thought and dialogue." Most important, I want to communicate that I take their concern, pressure, stress, or anxiety around their "problem" very seriously.

Furthering Talk

Question: What I was thinking about was the word *resonance.* The resonance in itself does not produce your responses. You are responsible for your responses and you have an active role. That's what I want you to elaborate on. When Tom said, quoting Wittgenstein, "See, don't think," he went on saying, for example, today, "I have a lot of thoughts in my inner dialogue, but I don't speak them." So he doesn't just see, he thinks at the same time and he makes choices. So each of us makes choices all the time, but... how to be responsive in making choices?

Harlene: I think this is an important question and also a complex question, in terms of being responsive. How do you know you're being responsive in a useful way, and by that I mean that you've heard the other person as best you can and that you're connecting with that person? You can never be 100%

sure, because you're always in the process of struggling with each other to try to understand and when you reach a point where you think there's a shared understanding...I think of it as you "think" there's a shared understanding but you can never really know. No matter how much we talk about the word *blue* or I try to respond to your descriptions or it, I may never be able to see the same blue or know that I'm seeing blue as you are. One of the things that I was thinking concerning Tom's comment about not thinking is that often the therapist's silent thinking slips into having silent interpretations or unspoken translations of what the other person is saying.

Question: How do you look upon the word *self*?

Harlene: Well, I think of the word *self* as a social construction that we have cultural, societal, philosophical, and theoretical constructions about. I'm more inclined to think of the idea of multiple selves, in contrast to the idea of the single core self, and in contrast to thinking of the idea that the self is inside, that a characteristic lies somewhere inside a person's body.

Question: How do you work with children?

Harlene: In my current work, to be quite honest, I don't work a lot with children. Somehow those kinds of families and people don't come to me these days. In the past I worked with children, and I have a paper that I co-authored with a colleague in a book called *Narrative Approaches to Children* in which we talk about working with children from a collaborative perspective and give a clinical example. My colleagues at the Houston Galveston Institute work with a lot with children, because most of the "problem situations" that are referred are families and children who are referred by the child welfare or the juvenile justice system.

One of our key principles is to always keep in mind that children are not just miniature adults and that we need to pay attention to the developmental stage that the child is in. When we're trying to develop a relationship with them, or relate with them or talk with them, we want to keep in mind that the way you try to engage with a 2-year-old is somewhat different from how you try to engage with a 6-year-old or an 8-year-old. When we have children in the session, we do not want to ignore them, talk "about" them as if they weren't present, or talk about them in an objectifying way. We want to include them in the conversation. We also want to keep in mind that children often communicate and express themselves in different ways than we do as adults.

Question: How does the idea of a philosophical stance being deep inside and something we can't learn fit with a postmodern, collaborative, mutually transforming therapy?

Harlene: My own experience as a therapist has been one of moving from seeing myself as the expert to one of seeing the client as the expert. When I said earlier that this is something you can't learn, let me back up and say that it's something that you cannot teach another person. My colleague Harry Goolishian used to say, "I cannot teach you how to be a therapist, but I can provide experiences and spaces in which you can learn to be a therapist." When I think of a philosophical stance, and I think of it as a worldview, a set of biases, values, and assumptions, I think that this is a choice that we make. The kind of philosophical stance I'm talking about might be appealing, attractive, or fitting for you, or it might not. However, that wouldn't be a choice or decision that I could make for you. You would make that for yourself: "This is something that's appealing, and this is something I want to incorporate in my life." That's where I come to the idea of the professional and the personal. For me, I don't separate my professional and my personal values.

Question: What are tentative manners?

Harlene: I did talk about tentative, and I talked about manners. Perhaps being tentative is an aspect of good manners. I hadn't thought about that. By tentative, I'm referring to the way I offer any comment, question, suggestion, gesture, to the attitude, the tone, manner, or mannerisms with which I offer it. An offering is provisional; I do not want to communicate that I think it is the truth or the reality. I always think of it as a contribution to the conversation; it is food for thought and dialogue; it is a way of participating in and fostering the conversation. It is not offered with the intent of directing the conversation, trying to sell an idea, or trying to privilege an outcome. No matter how strong our opinions are, and sometimes we do have strong opinions, I want to be open to being challenged and open that perhaps the other may not even be interested in talking about it at all. In other words, I must be willing to let it go.

Question: Could you expand on the ideas about the choices you make among the million things going on in your head as you're listening to the client? Which of your private thoughts do you choose to make public? How does one make an informed choice?

Harlene: As you're involved in a conversation, of course it's a spontaneous activity. It's sometimes challenging to slow yourself down, to not jump in and interrupt, and to take the time to think about what you might say next. Sometimes we get so drawn into a conversation that it's seductive not to be careful. One of the other things that your question makes me think about is this whole notion of the pause. In my book, I write about it as the Swedish or Scandinavian pause. Once I had a Swedish psychologist and social worker working with me in Houston, and they were fascinated and somewhat annoyed by how Texans talked over each other and past each other, not giving the other person the chance to finish, finishing their thought for them, or interrupting their train of thought. Their comments had a real profound effect on me. It was right about the same time that I heard Bateson comment that he always liked to have at least 7 seconds to think about his response. I think thoughtful responding requires giving the other person the time they need to say what they want to say, and to pause long enough to form your thoughts and your response to what they've said.

There are, as you said, a lot of choices that one can make in terms of what to respond to or what words to let come out of your mouth. Why do you respond to one word today, when if you could have the same conversation for the very first time tomorrow, you might hear it or respond to it differently? I have played with the idea of doing an "interview" with someone; call it a consultation, a therapy session, or having a conversation in which I would try to give an out-loud running commentary about my inner conversation and my spoken responses. In other words, I would try to explore why at that moment I made that particular comment. Of course, that process in itself would then influence what I respond to and how I respond. It's like watching a videotape of a therapy session, and each time you watch it, you have a different idea about why you chose to respond to one thing and not another. That's the best I can do at the moment. This is something that I think about a lot and will continue to think about.

Question: Could it sometimes be possible that the idea of "client as an expert" is only a declaration, and actually the person is working not along this guideline but in another context altogether. You might also use this as an excuse, kind of avoiding the responsibility of the therapist in a difficult situation. Can I get some of your comments to these ideas?

Harlene: Yes, sometimes it is difficult to articulate something in a way that you best convey the meaning or understanding about the concept you're hoping to convey. It's always a challenge. When I read something in a journal or a book chapter or hear something in a conference where someone has a different understanding of "the client is the expert" or "not-knowing" than I do, it's always a challenge for me to think about how to say it differently next time. Not that I want to correct the opinion or misunderstanding of the person who wrote it. I'm more concerned about the reader.

In the last part of your comment, the word that caught my attention was the word *responsibility.* This may not connect with your comment directly, but it's important for me. Sometimes we hear therapists talk about clients who aren't responsible or motivated, or who are resistant. Sometimes they even use some diagnostic terms for clients that they think aren't responsible. To some extent, we've created a psychotherapy culture where the therapist assumes, takes over, or gets in the way of the client being able to share in the responsibility. We do that by being experts. I really like John Shotter's idea of joint responsibility or shared responsibility. Certainly, as a therapist, I'm accountable for being the best therapist that I can, but I don't hold myself accountable for the client. I want to invite a relationship and process in which we can share accountability and responsibility for what we're doing. I want them to participate in holding me responsible, which goes back to my comment about research as part of everyday practice, and developing the habit of continually checking in with your client about how we're doing and how I'm doing.

Question: How you talk and negotiate with clients about the purpose and goals of therapy?

Harlene: I don't use the word *goals* for a couple of reasons. I want to keep in mind that what we think of as goals—that is, what the client hopes to accomplish and their expectations of me—is something that is fluid. It doesn't stay the same, it shifts through dialogue; it shifts along the way. I also don't think that people necessarily share the same goal, expectation, or hope. Each person involved in the conversation or the circumstances will have his or her own goal or variation of what may appear to be a shared one. There are at least as many outcomes, as many possibilities, as there are people involved in conversations and actions with each other around the "problem's" "solution." The challenge or the art is how to simultaneously work within all of those realities and be respectful of each.

Question: How do you comment on practice that you're not happy with?

Harlene: Let me respond to that by telling you a little bit about how a particular university program that I'm involved in works in terms of evaluation. I may come at this by the back door. First of all, my bias is that what we call theory and practice, they go hand in hand. My preference is to creating learning situations in which students do not first complete academic course work in the classroom and then go into the therapy room the second or the third year. I prefer that students simultaneously begin their course work and their practice work; these go hand in hand and inform each other.

The particular university program that I refer to is a psychology program in which all of the course work and practice is based in a postmodern social construction orientation. That is the culture that the students are introduced into and which they begin to live in throughout their study. The faculty is very open with our biases about the kinds of things that we think are important for the therapists to learn. Although there's a university course description or outline, each student also creates his or her own. Each student creates his or her own learning objectives or goals. Each student determines the way in which he or she wants to be evaluated. Do they want a multiple-choice exam, or do they want to write an essay? Do they want to have a conversation with the faculty? The evaluation can take any form and shape. This is very demanding for the faculty, to be able to meet multiple different kinds of learning agendas. The students get very excited about it. They get very involved in their own learning.

In the program, I have a clinical team that meets weekly— a group of six students—and I'm the supervisor. We meet for a year, and during that time we have three official evaluations. There's a university form or checklist that we must complete. There are some evaluation areas on it that I don't agree with and that I'm very open with the students about. The university form covers areas such as professionalism, relationships with clients, relationships with peers, skills and techniques, and integrating concepts and practice. I think of them as discussion questions, even though the form has a scale from 1 to 7. The way that most of the faculty use the form is as a beginning way to start talking about how the students are doing and how I'm doing. I always tell students that it is my job to help them be the best therapists that they can. I tell them, "If you don't make an 'A' when you're on my team, I have failed you." I also tell them that I need their help. I want to express an attitude that I am there to help them.

The evaluative process that I use is different than the way that evaluation is usually thought of in training or university programs. The students evaluate themselves, the supervisor evaluates the students, the students evaluate me, and I evaluate myself. We do this three times a year. We revisit what each student designated as their learning agenda as well as the learning agenda that the team collectively created for itself. Each student reflects on each of the other students, and each student offers a self-reflection. Each team member tells the others how they can help the member achieve his or her particular area of learning or growth. Additionally, I invite the students into a discussion about how we are doing as a team. "When you came to this team, what were you expecting? What were you hoping to learn; how were you hoping to grow and develop? What have you noticed in each other in terms of ways in which you've grown and evolved?" I think of these reflections and conversations as appreciative, looking at what we're doing well, what we want to enhance and do more of, and what we want to do differently.

Question: You referred to your work before as a "collaborative language systems" approach. What do you think about systems? What kind of systems are you referring to?

Harlene: When Harry and I originally became interested in language, we were inspired by the work at MRI (Mental Research Institute) and used language in the sense of what I call "using language strategically." If you could learn a client's language, meaning their words in the broadest sense, could conduct the session in the client's language, and could offer your comments in the client's language to make it short and a little bit simplistic, then there would be less resistance, more compliance, and more of an opportunity for change. How from this we became interested in language in a very different way is a very long story that took place over time. The more we tried to learn a client's language, the more we realized that each person in the room has his or her own unique language. The more you tried to learn, the more carefully you had to listen. This led to our having curiosities about the whole notion of language from a different angle.

That was the time in the late 1970s, when we first bumped into the Chilean biologists Maturana and Varela's ideas about language, and shortly thereafter started reading on hermeneutics. It was our early reading in hermeneutics that really began to introduce the idea about language and that human systems are meaning-making systems. We made a shift that was inspired by a conference that Tom had in Northern Norway where Harry had this "aha" experience that we had really moved in the direction of language systems and away from a cybernetic system metaphors. We talked about this idea first in the *Family Process* paper (1988) that Tom mentioned.

Question: You said you don't prefer, or you don't use, the word *goals.* You said you have customers coming from childcare agencies. How do you negotiate goals, how do you get common goals in conversations? About social control, how do you deal with social control?

Harlene: What I was hoping to say, when I said that I don't often talk about goals, or use that word, is that I don't think in terms of goals, in the way that we traditionally think about them in therapy, as something that's determined, fixed, as something we work toward, and there are particular strategies that you use to reach those. At the institute, we work a lot with what we call mandated or forced clients: clients that the law says have to come to therapy. When they send a referral to us, the child welfare agency will indicate who they're referring to therapy—in other words, who in the family they think needs therapy—and they will usually say what kind of therapy. For example, they might say one person needs individual therapy, a family needs family therapy, a mother needs group therapy, and they write their description of what the problem is and their goal on the referral form. In keeping with the idea that the client is the expert, and in a situation like this, the referring social worker or agency is a part of the system and is a client. The first thing that the therapist does is to talk to the social worker to learn more about the social worker's work with the family and its members to this point, his or her idea of designating individual therapy and family therapy, goals and expectations of the therapy, and equally important, what he or she has told the family or members of the family about being referred to us. The therapist then contacts some member of the family and talks to that person, saying, "You've been referred to us; this is what they've told us." The therapist talks with that member of the family about who he or she wants to come to the first meeting, and their ideas about it. It's a series of conversations, in which you're clarifying and elaborating on the conversation that's begun on paper, at least for us.

Each step of the conversation then informs the next. Sometimes the social workers are included in the therapy. We also involve the clients in . . . for example, we may say, "This is what child welfare wants you to accomplish in therapy. But if we can put that aside for a moment, we don't know if you even think that you should be here or you want to be here. What's happening in your family's life that you might want to talk about?" It's a process of inviting in their voice as the experts on themselves. With this particular work, because it involves legal court reports and there has to be documentation, the client and the therapist, together at the end of the session, write the progress notes. When a monthly report or final report has to be sent in, again, the client and the therapist together create the reports, and because the therapist has been in continued communication with the social worker, there aren't any surprises and people are usually, by that point, much more in agreement rather than in disagreement with each other. In working with mandated clients, because of the multiple realities and many strong opinions, and all of the institutional, societal, and political pulls, you can have some discrepant opinions and, what I've called in one paper a long time ago, "dueling realities."

Question: Thank you for telling us how you evaluate your students. I would like to ask you for your comments about how you evaluate the therapy, meaning did you achieve what you wanted or more, and did it work, and was it useful? Do you have some useful comments about that, and particularly how you do this in collaboration with your clients?

Harlene: Well, as I mentioned earlier, one of the things we value at the institute is a continual checking in or reflecting with our clients. "How am I doing? How are we doing? Is this useful? Would it be helpful to do something differently?" In other words, it's part of a therapy conversation. It depends on the therapist and the conversation at the moment; sometimes we check in at the beginning, sometimes during, and sometimes at the end of the session. Occasionally, maybe once every 2 years, the institute will develop a one-page form where clients can respond to their therapy and other aspects like coming to the institute, the receptionist, the telephone service, and those kinds of things. They may respond anonymously, or they may sign their name. Okay, one more question and then we'll go back to Bosnia.

Question: How do you negotiate the endings in the therapy?

Harlene: In my experience, clients tell you or let you know when they no longer need to come to therapy. Another way of thinking about it is that they let you know when you no longer need to be an active conversational partner in their life. They start doing what they want to in their lives, doing better, or feeling better, or simply having a sense that that's possible. If I'm working with a client and they seem to be doing very well, I'll say, "You know, we've been meeting now for so many times..." and I'll express my opinion of how I think they're doing. Hopefully, I'll first ask their opinion of how they think they're doing. We talk about it. Some clients might say, "I think I'm doing well and I don't think I need to come back again." Another client might be hesitant and I might say, "Well, rather than meeting every 2 weeks, how about meeting once a month from now on? Let's see how you do then." Another way of saying what I'm trying to say is, we talk about it.

Back to Bosnia

After the lunch break, Pat and I decided it was time to bring out the chocolates. There were smiles and laughter as each woman selected and savored her chocolate. During lunch Pat and I talked about the staff's requests, when they were helping us create the agenda. They had specific questions and topics that they wanted to cover, and they also wanted help with some of the women and families they were working with. So, we asked them if they'd like to use the afternoon to talk about their work. This would give us some of their real-life situations to refer to when addressing their questions and topics. All were eager to talk about their work. We asked them to divide into their teams and for each team to think of one of the women or situations that they were working on that they would want to share with the others and us for a consultation. After each team made a selection, I did what I often do when there is more than one person who wants a consultation: I asked each team to give a brief paragraph about what they would be talking about. We then asked for the whole group to decide which one they preferred to start with, which one seemed to be the most relevant to them. We also told them that we wanted to work with all of three of them, but we needed a starting point.

I will focus mostly on the process of the consultations and not the content or I'll never get to the last page of the story, which, of course, will really not be the end of the story. We used a different format for each story or consultation. Although the process was similar, the format had two common components. One, we wanted to make sure that we, Pat and I and their colleagues, understood the team members' agendas. What did *they* want from us? For example, did they want a general discussion? Did they have a particular question? Did they want fresh ideas? What were they hoping for? Again, in connection with your question about goals, it's very important to have a beginning sense of "Why are we talking about this? What are we hoping to accomplish, or at least we think or hope we're going to accomplish?" We asked the team members to talk with each other while the rest of us listened as they clarified their agenda. We wrote down what they wanted and double-checked our understanding with them. Two, we wanted to hear what the presenting team members thought would be important for us to hear, not what we or their colleagues thought important. We said to the presenting team, "*You* tell us what you think we need to know about this situation in order to be helpful to *you* with your agenda, with your hope or your expectations." We left it to the team to tell us what *they* thought we needed to know to be helpful. This is an important emphasis: The consultation is for the requesting persons, not the rest of us.

Before they began, we asked if we could make a request of their colleagues who would be listening to their story. We asked the listening colleagues, "Listen to your colleagues' story about their work, pay careful attention to what *they are telling us that they* want from the consultation, what *they* want help with, and pay careful attention to their story. However, we want to listen to it as if you are a member of the story; for instance, the mother, the wife, the dead son, or the grandmother." We also said that although they, like Pat and me, may be eager to ask a question or make a comment, to please put them on hold. We told the presenters that after they finished with their story, we would ask them if they would like to hear their listening colleagues' reflections.

We then let the team members collectively tell their story in the manner they chose. We gave them ample time to talk. When there were pauses that seemed like stopping places, we would ask, "Is there anything more you want to tell us? Is this enough?" When they signaled that they had finished, we asked if they wanted to hear their colleagues' reflections. Yes, they indicated. We then asked the members of each of the two listening teams—again, we had included one of the guests in each—to reflect with each other on the story they had just heard while their presenting colleagues listened. We also asked them to keep in mind what the presenting team had requested of us. After the reflecting process, Pat and I first asked the team presenters to share reflections with each other about their colleagues' reflections. We then had a conversation with them about their reflections and a discussion about their experience of the consultation, including how it was or how they imagined it might be helpful or not.

We began each consultation with the same requests of the presenters and the reflectors. After the story paused, however, the listening colleagues' reflecting processes took different shapes, as we offered options for variations from which they could choose. That is a quick description of the skeletal framework and the general format of the consultations.

Again, very important in my work is people having the time and space they need to say what they want to say, and others being able to be in a listening position. If Pat and I had an idea or a question when we talked to the presenters about their experience, their ideas of the reflections, it was offered as a way of participating in the conversation with them. We did not have an agenda of highlighting one thing as more useful than another or moving the team in any particular consensus or action direction. I think of this as a polyphonic process, a collective storytelling and generation of ideas. That is, the team, much like family members, collectively tell the story, each putting in her own pieces. The reflecting listeners and the facilitators also add to the story's development. In my experience, the kind of process that I just described gives the opportunity for participants' voices to come to the center, as they become aware of, appreciate, and begin to develop their own local knowledge, expertise, and competence. The consultant as the expected knower or the expert begins to fade into the background.

After the third consultation, we reached the end of a very long and full day. The air, however, was filled with energy. Later that evening, over dinner, Pat and I, of course, talked about the day and our experience of the shift in the women in terms of their level of energy and enthusiasm and their sense of hope by the end of the first day. Some of the things that we noticed were the following: In listening to the presentations, it was obvious that staff had a wealth of experience, expertise, creativity, and dedication that they didn't give themselves credit for. One of the groups, I don't remember exactly how they did it, but they very creative in their reflections, as they went back to the earlier morning discussion about "hope" and "hopeful" and used some of the words and phrases that had come up in the conversational clusters. In the discussions following the consultations, there was a subtle sense that they were talking less about the women and their families as objectified objects and isolated entities. It had become apparent to us that they were used to working more with the individual women and not other members of the family, particularly the male members or others who lived in the same house. They had begun to broaden their ideas about ways in which to approach violence and have conversations with people about violence, and they were beginning to wonder what the other family voices could offer. Partly, the curiosity about other voices was influenced by the "as if" listening-reflecting process.

Pat and I wondered over dinner how the staff might continue to build on or pull together their experiences and talents in a way that would be useful to them as a staff and to their clients. What was becoming obvious was that this was a group of competent, talented, and creative women. We thought—maybe it was a way of reorganizing or formalizing what they were doing in some way—it was almost like the pieces were there, but could they be shifted or moved in some way to create a different picture or a different backdrop from which they could do their work. One of our last thoughts, probably after several glasses of wine, was wondering what their dreams were—what dreams did they have about their work? That is, in our thinking about the hopes that they had expressed the day before, we started talking about dreams. When we came in the next day, the women looked different. They were dressed, for lack of another way to describe it, more special; they had more presence and more life in their eyes. We again acknowledged what we had learned from them the day before about the challenges they faced in their work, being burned out, overwhelmed, and so forth. We went back to their agenda list and had a discussion of some the items and questions, using the three consultations from the day before to tie ideas to content. They were quickly developing fresh ideas about their work.

After the coffee break, we told them about our conversation over dinner and that we had wondered about their dreams. We asked them if they'd be willing to have "dreaming conversations" with each other. They were a little curious or teased by our idea, so they moved into three conversational clusters, again requesting that a guest join each one. We originally thought that about 30 minutes would be ample time but the room was abuzz. They talked and talked and talked and didn't want to stop. Finally, at 45 minutes we were able to get them to pause and "officially" reconvene as the large group, and it was amazing what they had talked about. I say officially because the three groups had overheard each other's conversations and had begun to talk with each other.

They had an amazing dream. They had the idea that they were going to create a women's center that would offer all kinds of programs and services for women *and* their families *and* their children. They would go to the women themselves and ask them what kind of programs and services they wanted. They had also decided that they would go to the other nongovernmental organizations in town and to the city government officials and talk with them about their ideas. Specifically, they wanted to have a 24-hour hotline, parenting groups, and playgroups. And they had the idea that the women they served could come together and knit things that they would then sell to make money. They were much energized. Basically what they were saying was that they would go to the women and the community for information and feedback. They had also decided that to accomplish this, each team would have an assignment.

Each team would have to be accountable for carrying out an aspect of getting the center and its programs going. I silently wondered if maybe their idea was a little ambitious, given the number of staff that they were and what they wanted to do. So, I asked out loud: Did they already feel overworked? How could they make it work? What ideas did they have? They said, "Perhaps we can use volunteers, but how? We don't know anything about volunteers. Where would we get them? How would we train them?" All of a sudden I thought, "Aha!" The translator had been in all the conversational clusters and had become involved in all the conversations and the development of the ideas. I said, "Perhaps you have your very first volunteer here in the room." I was remembering that the volunteer was a woman without a job and, according to her, she had no prospect of having a job. When I said that perhaps they had their very first volunteer, the woman just lit up! It never occurred to her, she was there as the translator and having a good time. This started a whole new conversation about volunteers and what their resources for volunteers and other things were.

We took a lunch break and this day, rather than Pat and I going to lunch by ourselves, the staff invited us to join them in ordering lunch from their favorite little stand around the corner that made sausage sandwiches. They suggested that Pat and I have one of the sandwiches. This seemed to be their lunchtime ritual. We paid for our own food, of course. Remember, these were women who hadn't been paid their salaries for 3 months.

They were in and out of the room and talking with each other during lunch. I went into the office area for lunch and being "Nosy Rosy," I picked up a fold-over pamphlet that was written in Bosnian that had the staffs' photo on the front. So, I asked the secretary in the office (she spoke English) what it said. Well, to my surprise it was an announcement of the "Women's Center" and its services. I was baffled; they already had a center?

When we reconvened after lunch, there was a marked silence. Pat and I sat there and took in the silence, each of us silently wondering what was going on, when all of a sudden one of the women blurted out, "Are you serious?" Pat and I almost simultaneously looked at each other and said, "Are we serious about what?" Another one said, "This is so touching about our new program, or is this just an exercise?" We were just speechless. We would never have imagined that they thought we were not serious. I told them, "To the contrary! I'm usually accused of being too serious." Pat and I expressed our genuine interest and support of their ideas and what they could do.

I then posed my curiosity about the pamphlet that I saw in the office. Well, it seems that although the official name is a center, they associated the word *center* with a physical location where services could be offered. The building they were in was not a center because it didn't have space for people. People usually came to the "center" only to see the doctor who came from Sarajevo once a week. Otherwise, they offered their services in the women's homes.

We next had a general discussion about how to "fine-tune" their idea about a new "center." They came up with some further ideas. We had them go back to the small groups and talk more about the kind of information they would need to know: what kinds of services to offer, how they would gather the information, and who in the community they would need to talk with. They had used the word *publicity*, so we said, "What kind of publicity do you want to have?"

Again, when they came back, we were amazed at their creativity and their energy. We had a general discussion about the ideas that had emerged in this last round of conversations. One of the topics that surfaced was about naming things. What would they name the program? What did they want the name to convey? Who would they invite to participate in the naming?

They had discussions about how to continue the momentum and the commitment to their new ideas and about the resource opportunities in the community. They were also concerned about the London office, so we talked about that concern with them. They wondered what the London office would say about their plan. They feared: Would the London office allow them to do it? The discussion turned to the writing of a report that Pat had been requested by the London office to send to them following the consultation and training. We discussed with the women what they thought would be the important things to put in the report for the London office. So, while we were there that week, Pat started to draft a report about the first part of our work for the London office, and she was back and forth in conversation with the women about it. We spent the next 2 days, as I mentioned earlier, in the field accompanying the staff on their visits to work with the women and their families in their homes. We continued to address their questions and interests from the first day's agenda, although, as is often the case, some of the importance of our "perceived expertise" diminished as they accessed their own competencies and created their own answers. We also went with them to the Commemorative Center, which I mentioned earlier.

About 6 months later, Pat went back to do another training by herself and she told me that they were following through with many of the things that they had planned, which was very exciting to hear. To make a long story short, before coming here, which would have been about a year later, I found out that the program had been closed. There was no more money from London, so they couldn't continue the program or fully create the women's center. What good is a consultation or training for a dead program? Who does it help?

I do not think of the outcome or the product of the consultation as a new program or a new center that never fully materialized. Instead, I think of it as helping women who created local knowledge and expertise and who accessed and broadened their competencies. They did not create concrete, final, ongoing solutions, but they developed a sense that possibilities exist. In this process, their connections and relationships with each other and with their clients and colleagues in the community became stronger. One woman said, after the consultation when Pat was back 6 months later, "We used our experience with you as a model for working with our beneficiaries and for others in the community." *Beneficiaries* is the language they use, I'm using the word *clients*.

In closing, each woman created new meanings for her life, a new way of experiencing herself, a new sense of competency, a sense of feeling helpful and hopeful. I have full trust that this newness will live on for each of the women and will be carried with them in other areas of their life and future work, and in turn will help others whose lives they touch. I carry these women and newness with me also.

International Outsider Thoughts

Yishai Shalif: When referring to the question of what is the most important thing about being a therapist, Harlene used the term *good manners*. Later she spoke of the importance of anything offered by the therapist should be in a *tentative manner*. Someone in the audience put these two concepts together and introduced the term *good tentative manners*. Harlene responded saying she has not thought of that before; however, she sees it as related to what she thinks as "an offering that is food for thought and dialogue."

As someone born to a mother who was originally British, the term *good manners* is one that resonates for me. I found this term especially reverberating while reading about the work in Bosnia when Harlene and Pat responded when they were struck by the heavy mood emotions in the room and the use of the words *hopeless* and *helpless*. The tentative and tender introduction into the room of their reflection on what was happening in their eyes, and the careful anchoring of this reflection in the language of the women, seemed to me an excellent example of good tentative manners.

It evoked the image of the Jewish custom of Shiva (the 7 days in which people come to sit with people who have lost their dear ones and console them). This is usually a solemn practice that centers the bereaved in a very tentative manner. One waits for them to open the conversation and choose the topics to talk about. One is there to hear about the stories of the deceased, but is also open to hear other stories.

Talking to people who have suffered a loss or other hardship is not an easy task, at least for me. I feel it needs courage. The same goes for raising difficult issues in therapy. I'm always in debt to one of my first supervisors, Dr. Esther Cohen, who encouraged me to "not be afraid" to ask questions that one may recoil from. Looking back to her encouragement, I find that the tentative manner that she had with me has made it possible for me to adopt it as a regular practice.

Another dimension to this anecdote referring to Harlene and Pat's work is not only the courage to speak about the difficult parts, but also the ability to point out aspects of a conversation that may not be in the forefront. The women did not talk directly about wanting to deal with hopelessness and helplessness. It was through Harlene and Pat's observation that they, in a tentative manner, brought it up. It reminds me of my work with a young man aged 17. I love to work with him and have conversations with him. A few times while having these conversations, the overt talk could be positive and hopeful, but somehow his face spoke a different language. When, in a tentative manner, I offered this observation, it opened incredible new and refreshing venues for the conversation.

John Gurnaes: Talking about the client as the expert Harlene says, "When I refer to the client as the expert, I'm referring to the client as the expert on his or her life. The client is the expert on his or her story and the content of the story. The client is the expert on what's important and what's not important to talk about. When I think of the client as the expert, that makes me the learner. The client is my teacher, and

I'm learning from the client. In my experience, when you're genuinely interested in the person and curious about that person and try to learn about that person, I have found that that naturally invites them into a shared or mutual inquiry or joint activity. In other words, what might be thought of as starting out as a one-way process, the therapist learning from the client, naturally shifts to a two-way process in which they're engaged in learning together."

The position from where the therapist learns and participates in this collaborative inquiry is the "not-knowing position." But not knowing is not a not-knowing but is a knowing created within the ongoing exchange of dialogue. "Not-knowing refers to the way that I think about knowing, the way that I think about what I know or what I think I might know, and the intent with which I use or author that knowledge." In this way the concept of not-knowing is also an invitation to the therapist to take a kind of reflective distance from his or her own knowledge. This is not the same as having therapeutic dialogue, where the therapist is operating from hidden private ideas, thoughts, or questions. From Harlene's perspective, therapeutic dialogues are about finding ways of making private ideas, thoughts, or questions visible and useful as "food for the dialogue." This is an intention that invites taking a reflective distance to these knowledges. To find ways to go public with inner conversations, ideas, and thoughts in the dialogue is a safeguard against slipping into what you might punctuate as a monological conversation in your own head.

I don't think it is difficult for most therapists to recognize dialogue, as Harlene talks about dialogue, as a conversational position in their work. But dialogues are always in danger of collapsing into monologues or into what Bakhtin calls monological dialogues. Bakhtin defines dialogues as open-ended conversations and monological dialogues as conversations where participants in the conversations stay within their own monologues. I think most therapists sometimes find themselves enthusiastically carried away by their own ideas, or find themselves being so "respectful" that clients keep within their own monologues. I will stay a bit with Harlene's community work in Bosnia, because I think it is a good illustration of how to keep therapeutic conversations as dialogues.

What struck me in the beginning of Harlene's story about her experiences in Bosnia was how easy it would have been to impose a lot of expert knowledge on the Bosnian staff group, as has been the tradition in Western psychological intervention models. Instead, Harlene and Pat moved into a mutual inquiry with the staff that invited them, as well as Harlene and Pat, to learn from and see the "life" of the staff through the eyes of the members. Of course, this inquiry started out as a one-way process. It was very important because it brought forward very personal as well as common stories and knowledges which, I think, were impossible to predict beforehand. This is one of the really important outcomes of conversations wherein therapists or community workers position themselves as learners. Something unexpected for the client/participants as well as for the therapist/community worker almost always comes out of such inquiries. This is what prepares the ground for further conversations or inquiries that stay closely connected to participants' experiences and sense of what is important to them.

What, to me, really brought the Bosnian groups' painful monologues or monological dialogues into a two-way process or dialogue was Harlene and Pat's invitation to talk about hope. They said, "It's one thing to think about how to approach something where you feel you can't help and there's no hope versus approaching something where you feel that maybe you can help, maybe you can hope." By responding to the staff's strong sense of hopelessness and helplessness in this way, Harlene and Pat stepped into the conversation as dialogical partners. To me, this is a very good example of how community workers and therapists, by their responses, can step into and move a conversation from a one-way to a two-way process and thus into a dialogue. It's not about imposing something on someone or about being passive, but about being a collaborative partner in a conversation in a way that moves the talk into new territories of the "client's life." These territories are of importance to the "clients" and at the same time have relevance to the purpose of the meeting.

I feel easily connected to the way Harlene talks about the client as an expert, the not-knowing position, to the way she talks about dialogue and her collaborative approach to therapy. But I really became confused when she, at the beginning of her presentation, talked about her philosophical stance as a therapist and as a person.

About the position from where Harlene acts as a therapist and a person, she says, "I'm often asked, well how can you learn to take this philosophical stance? My reply is usually, I'm not sure that you can learn to do this. It has to be something that you sincerely believe and value, and it fits for you deep inside. If that is the case, then you will find yourself spontaneously, genuinely, and naturally acting in particular ways."

I must admit that I was surprised that a postmodernist would restore, and bring herself into, one of the big romantic narratives about the therapist in this way. To talk about real therapists' actions in therapy as an expression of a certain spontaneous genuinely natural being, independent of practices, skills, theories, techniques, and experiences that the therapist has acquired or developed in his or her training, professional and personal life, seems to be an expression of a being from nowhere. It's a restoration of the "big romantic narrative" about therapists that is well known, among others, from Rogers's client-centered and nondirective therapy. The difference is that in Harlene's narrative, such a being seems to be out of our reach, in the sense that it is something we can't learn or can't be taught. I really wondered why she restored such a narrative and at the same time mystifies the therapist's position and brought the "successful therapist" back into a power position.

This drew me into thinking about some of the dilemmas that have grown out of describing the therapist's position as not-knowing and not-influential. By this I am referring to a way of thinking about the therapist's position in the tradition that Harlene is a part of and I feel myself connected to. This tradition grew out of an interest in parts of the field of family therapy to move away from first-order cybernetics and the dominant strategic and structural traditions within the field. Therapists within this tradition became interested in Heinz von Foerster's second-order cybernetics, Maturana's ideas about autopoiesis. They became interested in the philosophy of language, in Harry Goolishian's and Harlene Anderson's redefinition of human systems from cybernetic into linguistic and meaning-making systems. This marked a "linguistic turn" in this influential part of the field of family therapy, as well as more recently in social constructionism, postmodernism, and poststructuralism. The tradition "robbed" the therapist from any privileged access to true knowledge about reality and their clients, and it "robbed" the therapist of the power to change their clients in a strategic unidirectional way. Instead it became the job of the therapist, within this tradition, to not be an agent of change but rather to leave power and control behind, for the purpose of making it possible for clients to change themselves in a way and direction that they wanted.

I wonder how is it possible to talk about therapeutic techniques, methods, practices, and skills in a way that makes clients change by themselves and at the same time argue against talking about therapists as strategic agents of change? This dilemma was resolved by talking about therapy on an abstract meta-theoretical, philosophical, or epistemological level. But this is not the same thing as doing therapy in everyday practice. There is simply a distance in talking about autopoiesis, philosophy of language, dialogues, and so on, and to be in a therapeutic relationship with a family where sexual abuse is on the agenda, or with a refugee who has been subjected to severe torture and loss or with a girl who is about to die because she does not eat. But because of the effort of this tradition not to put the therapist in a position as a "strategic agent of change" or in a "knowing position," there has been a reluctance within the tradition to talk about knowledges, practices, techniques, and skills that make such therapies effective and successful. Not to talk about such achievements as an expression of certain knowledges, skills, practices, and techniques leads to either think about such achievements as spontaneous achievements of clients, which then makes therapists and therapy training irrelevant, or to think about such achievements as expressions of a mystical and special gifted being from out of nowhere. This paradoxically brings the successful therapist back into a power position. In this way it seems impossible to escape bringing the therapist into a position where he or she has power to influence what is going on in therapy in a way that makes therapy either successful or unsuccessful. So the question is then not if the therapist has influence on what is going on in therapy, but how the therapist influences the therapy in a way that makes therapy successful and helpful to clients.

I think Harlene's words that the therapist is an *expert* on the processes marks an interesting entry into conversation about what makes successful therapies successful. I also think that the presentation of her work with the Bosnian group expressed knowledges about processes, as well as practices, that could be very interesting to explore further. Such inquiries would resolve a dilemma which I as an "insider" consider to be a serious dilemma within the tradition. So, thank you for that entry.

Harlene's Response

Dear Yishai and John,

I appreciate your thought-provoking and dialogue-inviting reflections. I also appreciate this opportunity to continue our dialogue. What caught my attention before I read your reflections was the word *outsider.* Might we think of it as participating in the conversation from a different position?

Yishai, thank you for highlighting the notion of "good tentative manners." I will give more thought to this idea: How to be genuinely polite but not so polite that the "other" experiences you as insincere or feels uncomfortable with your words and actions. Thank you also for reminding us of the Jewish Shiva, the listener waiting for the speaker and being open to the speaker's choosing. I had not thought of using this example in my teaching, but I will in the future.

Yes, there are various ways that our clients communicate with us, and I cannot overstate the importance of our being aware of those ways in the moment. This invites the question of, if and when to respond to what we imagine we are receiving. And how, in a tentative manner, can we "check out" our interpretations, our hunches, and so forth of what we think the other is communicating. With my students, I emphasize "checking out" as exploring to learn rather than exploring to confirm. I also emphasize the risk of making private hypotheses or judgments about what is sometimes referred to as nonverbal behavior or unconscious speaking through our bodies and then privately operating from these.

John, thank you for sharing your surprise and comments about the philosophical stance and the professional and the personal, and for the thoughts that followed. You pose important and complex discussions that I continuously engage in with myself and others.

If I understood your concerns, I don't mean to imply that I think the therapist is not in a position of influence. I think that we are always in a position of influence. However, I also think that influence is mutual; I am affected by the client as well. Regarding my participation in influencing, I want to be cautious that I do not, wittingly or unwittingly, affect a conversation, and thus a client, toward what I might "expertly" determine as a preferred direction or outcome. I also don't mean to imply a romanticized notion of the therapist, perhaps, quite the opposite.

We take all of who we are with us into the therapy room—for example, our histories, our experiences, our biases, and our preferences—it is impossible to leave it behind. Given this, I want to have the capacity to invite particular relationship and conversation spaces and processes that have the potential for generativity. This therapist capacity is what I want to foster. I do not think that this is accomplished by learning and applying sets of skills and techniques to clients as we traditionally think of in psychotherapy. At the same time, I do not think in terms of "spontaneous achievements" or "a mystical and special gifted being from out of nowhere," implying that therapists and therapy training are irrelevant. I erred when I said, "I'm not sure that you can *learn* to do this." What I want to emphasize is that I question our orientation to "training" therapists. I am very interested in what makes any therapy event successful or not, and most importantly, from the client's experience and description. From what I have learned over the years from interviewing clients about their experiences of therapy and therapists is that what they determine successful, in my opinion, is not that related to therapist punctuations like skills and techniques.

Now, I am biased. I have, as each of us does, preferences for how we think about therapy and our roles as therapists. As I mentioned, at the heart of mine is the "philosophical stance." In my experience, if one believes in the assumptions associated with the stance, that belief will inform the way of being that I suggest becomes natural and spontaneous. Take, for instance, "the client is the expert" on his or her life. I do not think that I can teach a therapist to believe that the client is the expert. This is not a teachable skill or technique. Taking such a participatory stance requires us to reorient ourselves to how we think of expertise, knowledge, and our engagement as therapists, among other things. What the expertise is that I think therapists from my persuasion bring and how to create environments in which this can be learned—and to be learned, it has to fit, and not just intellectually but in the heart and the gut—is a worthy discussion that I would like to have with you and others on an occasion when time and space permits. Once again, thank you.

4

Scaffolding a Therapeutic Conversation

MICHAEL WHITE

Michael White was the Director of the Adelaide Narrative Therapy Centre in Adelaide, South Australia, which is a center for narrative therapy and community work. He originally trained in social work and family therapy, developing new and original ideas and practices out of dissatisfaction with many of ways of thinking and working traditionally found in those fields. He was the most prolific and influential figure in the development of narrative therapy. Professor Karl Tom says about White, "As a therapist he was an applied deconstruction activist." In his life, Michael liked swimming, biking, and flying the sport plane.

The Endurance of Stalled Initiatives

My plan is to share with you a story about a therapeutic conversation. In this story you will meet a young man whose name is Colin, and his mother, Martha. There is also a referring therapist, Judy, and me. This therapeutic conversation occurred in a consultation interview in a small workshop situation, and the history is that Colin has been in lots of trouble, principally because of episodes of going on a rampage and destroying property. He has spent a lot of time in detention centers as a result of this. At the time of this consultation interview, Colin is in a medium security detention center, which is a rustic, rural environment. He's now 12 years of age, going on 13, and Judy, who'd been meeting with him recently, had noticed an interesting development in his life. In this development, Colin had handled his frustration by walking out on a deck attached to the detention center cafeteria instead of lashing out at people and smashing things. Judy regarded this to be an extraordinary initiative, as, in response to experiencing frustration, it was usual for Colin to run amok.

Judy was worried that Colin's initiative in dealing with frustration in this way could easily be lost, and she was hoping that in this consultation interview this initiative could serve as a point of entry to the development of an alternative storyline about Colin's life. She was also hoping that this would provide a foundation for Colin to take further steps of a similar nature. Further, it was Judy's hope that the consultation interview would provide an opportunity to further develop the mother–son alliance. This alliance had been disrupted by the circumstances of Colin and Martha's lives.

Judy's appreciation of Colin's initiative in walking out on the deck when frustrated, and her understanding that this initiative of Colin's might provide a point of entry to the development of an alternative storyline of his life, resonated strongly for me. It is my understanding that one is likely to have a good life when only 97% of one's initiatives in living are stalled. Let me explain. It seems quite clear that people are always making initiatives in living, but that very few of these survive. Very few of them endure. It is my estimation that when 3% of one's initiatives of living survive, one can expect to experience a reasonably good quality of life. However, when 98% of one's initiatives in living are lost, when only 2% survive, one can expect to experience a relatively poor quality of life. This leads me to the conclusion that, as therapists, we have a role to play in the unstalling of, and in supporting the endurance of, 1% of people's initiatives in living.

I believe that this is very significantly what the skills of therapeutic practice are about. In the context of narrative practice, a small percentage of the ever-present but otherwise neglected initiatives of people's lives are identified, characterized, acknowledged, honored, and taken into the development of storylines that have been subordinated by the dominant and often problem-saturated stories of people's lives. I am using the term *initiative* as a substitute for the terms *exception* and *unique outcome*, because this term evokes a sense of personal agency, that is, a sense that one has the capacity to play a part in the shaping of one's own actions and the sense that, in some way, the world is responsive to the fact of one's existence.

There are many ways of contributing to the characterization and acknowledgment of these neglected initiatives. One option is to support people in the development of a rich account of the foundation of these initiatives. This is a foundation that features specific knowledge about life and skills of living that people have developed in the history of their lives. What people give value to in their lives, and what they intend for their lives, is also part of the foundation of these initiatives. The development of a rich account of these types of knowledge and skills, of what people accord value to, and of what they intend for their lives is achieved through the careful scaffolding of the therapeutic conversation.

This term *scaffolding* is drawn principally from the work of the followers of the Russian psychologist, Lev Vygotsky, and is related to the metaphor of "construction." When taken up as a concept of therapeutic practice, scaffolding refers to the therapist's contribution in providing a context for people to separate from what is known and familiar to them about their lives and to arrive at what it might be possible for them to know about their lives, and to do. In contributing this scaffolding, the therapist does not engage in "pointing out positives," "giving affirmations," "illustrating strengths and resources," "reframing" the difficult experiences of people's lives, "making hypotheses," or "delivering interventions." Rather, the therapist initiates the sort of inquiry that makes it possible for people to traverse the gap between what is known and familiar to them and what it is possible for them to know and to do. This scaffolding provides people with support in the incremental and progressive distancing from the known and familiar toward what it is possible for them to know and to do. Without the assistance of this scaffolding, this gap between the known and familiar and what it is possible to know and to do represents and impassable chasm or gulf.

Vygotsky referred to this gap as the *zone of proximal development* (Vygotsky, 1986). Before returning to the story of Colin and Martha, I will provide a summary of Vygotsky's observations about this zone.

The Zone of the Proximal Development

Vygotsky was interested primarily in explorations of early childhood development. In these explorations, he determined that in a great majority of cases, development is founded on learning. This was a challenge to much of the prevailing developmental theory of his time, which asserted that development preceded learning; that learning was the outcome of the unfolding of some genetic or neurological imperative.

Vygotsky sought to reveal the genesis of this learning that provided the conditions for development, and his research brought him to the following conclusions:

1. Learning is the outcome of social collaboration. In this social collaboration, skilled caretakers and sophisticated peers provide supported learning tasks that are within the reach of the child but that require the investment of significant effort on behalf of the child.
2. It is through these learning tasks that children have the opportunity to distance from the immediacy of their experience of the world. This is a movement toward what they might know and do in collaboration with others.
3. This was a movement across a zone of learning that he called the *zone of proximal development*. Vygotsky defines the zone of proximal development as "the distance between the actual developmental level as determined by independent problem solving and the level of potential development as determined through problem solving under adult guidance or in collaboration with more capable peers." (1986, p. 86)
4. In this movement across this zone, there is a shift from gathering the objects and events of the world into "heaps" in which the child unites diverse objects and events in groups under a common family name, to gathering the objects and events of the world into chains of association, or into complexes, that establish bonds and relations between these objects and events.
5. There are several levels in the development of these chains of association or formation of complexes, from the preliminary

unification of objects and events on the basis of maximum similarity to the grouping of objects and events on the basis of a single attribute (e.g., only round objects or flat objects).

6. This development of complex thinking provides a foundation for the development of concepts. To quote Vygotsky, the development of a concept "presupposes more than unification. To form such a concept it is also necessary to abstract, to single out elements, and to view the abstracted elements apart from the totality of the concrete experience in which they are embedded." (1986, p. 135)

7. This conceptual development provides a foundation for children to intervene in the shaping of their own actions and in the shaping of their lives. According to Vygotsky, on account of this development, children are now able to operate with these concepts at will and as a task demands, and with a consciousness of these operations, understanding them to be processes of a certain kind. In Vygotsky's terms, it is this development that leads to self-mastery in intellectual functions: For example, he asserts that this concept development is the foundation of "deliberate attention, logical memory, abstraction, the ability to compare and to differentiate" (Vygotsky, 1986, p. 86). In terms that I prefer, this development of conceptual thought is the foundation of personal agency. It is through the development of these concepts that children begin to inhabit their own lives.

8. Language and word meaning evolution is crucial to this conceptual development. The pathway to concept formation is the development of word meanings. To quote Vygotsky again: "When a new word has been learned by the child, its development is barely starting; as the child's intellect develops, it is replaced by generalizations of a higher and higher type—a process that leads in the end to the formation of true concepts. . . . Real concepts are impossible without words, and thinking in concepts does not exist beyond verbal thinking. That is why the central movement in concept formation, and its generative cause, is a specific use of words as functional tools." (1986, p. 107)

Vygotsky's understanding of the part that social collaboration and language play in development is also underscored by his assertion that the private speech of young children, sometimes referred to as "ego-centric speech" or "speech for oneself," is social in its origins. This development of private speech is achieved through the scaffolding of the child's proximal zone of development, and it reflects the development of the child's capacity to distance from the immediacy of his or her experience and to reflect on the objects and events of his or her world. This development of private speech is also reflective of the child's engagement with problem-solving culture.

This private speech becomes more condensed and cryptic in the fifth and sixth years of life because it is moving underground and becoming the language of inner life. Vygotsky proposes that this language of inner life provides us with a sense of self. According to this conception, the self is social and relational in its origins: This is a sense of self that is derived from inner experience that is founded on the internalization of private speech.

The Zone of Proximal Development and Therapeutic Practice

In his research, Vygotsky focused on early childhood learning. But the considerations relating to the zone of proximal development are relevant for learning at all stages and ages. And I believe these considerations to be highly relevant to the development of therapeutic practice.

In a great many instances, people consult therapists when they are having difficulty in proceeding with their lives; in these circumstances, in their efforts to address their predicaments and concerns, people are reproducing the known and the familiar. The gap between this known and familiar and what it is possible for people to know and to do can be considered a zone of proximal development. This zone cannot be traversed without the sort of conversational partnership that would provide the necessary scaffolding to achieve this; that is, the sort of scaffolding that would provide the opportunity for people to traverse this zone in manageable steps. In this conversational partnership, it is the therapist's role to contribute to the scaffolding of the proximal zone of development.

It is this scaffolding that makes it possible for people to incrementally and progressively distance from the known and familiar toward what it might be possible for them to know and to do. It is this scaffolding that supports people in the formation of chains of association or complexes, and in the development of concepts about life and about identity. It is this scaffolding that makes it possible for people to arrive at what it is possible for them to know about their lives and identities, and that gives them a foundation for proceeding to address the predicaments and concerns of their lives.

The Story of Colin and Martha*

Colin is young man who usually has very few words in his conversation with adults. He is generally considered incapable of reflecting on his life, unable to foresee the consequences of his actions, and relatively incapable of taking responsibility for his own life. He is judged to be a concrete thinker, without a capacity to think in abstract terms.

It is my understanding that the development of a capacity for Colin to reflect on his own life, to foresee the consequences of his actions, to take responsibility for his life, and to think in abstract terms would be the outcome of careful attention to the scaffolding of his zone of proximal development. This is the sort of scaffolding that helps one to incrementally and progressively distance from the known and familiar toward what it is possible for one to know about one's world. This is the sort of scaffolding that I endeavored to provide in my therapeutic conversation with Colin and Martha.

As a way of illustrating the scaffolding of my conversation with Colin and Martha, I will provide a transcript of a significant piece of this conversation. This transcript is from a point approximately 20 minutes into the conversation. I have already given some account of what I learned in this first 20 minutes about Colin's history of running amok, of his incarceration, of the disruption of his relationship with his mother, of his initiative in walking out on the deck of the cafeteria, and of the hopes that Judy had for the consultation. In this first

---

* To protect client confidentiality, the editors have done their best to de-identify both persons and context.

20 minutes I also learned that Martha had recently secured accommodation in a small apartment and that this had presented Colin with some opportunities for 'weekend release" to stay with her.

On hearing about the initiative of walking out on the deck, I ask Martha and Colin if it would be okay by them for us to talk more about this development. In response to this question, Martha says, "Well I don't mind. I'm not trying to be facetious but I don't know how I can talk about that anymore because we just did. I wouldn't know how to expand on that."

M: Well I could certainly ask a lot of questions because I'm quite intrigued by these developments. Would that work for you?

Martha: Yeah.

M: Or do you have some other thoughts about what you'd like to talk about today?

Martha: No, I was kind of hoping that you'd do your thing (laughter).

M: What about you, Colin, did you have any special thoughts about what you'd like to talk about today?

Colin: No.

M: Okay, all right. So maybe we can pick up a little bit on some of Judy's ideas for our talk. Would that be okay? Because she's come up with an idea about what it would be good to talk about. So shall we pick that up?

Martha: Yeah, okay, so you go ahead. I'm here to observe too, you know (laughter).

M: I just wonder, Colin, Judy talked about how you were taking strides in a positive direction—those were her words—and particularly since August. Do you know what she's talking about? Does that ring a bell for you?

Colin: Yep. I've been behaving a lot better.

M: Okay. What does behaving a lot better mean, like what . . .

Colin: Like staying in group and following through.

M: Following through.

Colin: And taking space when I need it.

M: Following through, taking space when you need it.

Colin: Mmm, hm.

M: And staying in group, did you say?

Colin: Yeah.

M: What does "staying in group" mean?

Colin: Well, when you're part of the group like everyone else. It's all right then. When you're in group you can go to the movies, right.

M: Yeah, okay.

Colin: But if you're out of group, you don't do anything. You just go down the hill and you talk about your issues. About why you're out of group and about how you could have done better. And sometimes you can spend 3 to 4 days down there.

M: Okay, so you get special privileges like going to the movies, and other stuff as well?

Colin: Yes.

M: So you get special privileges when you are staying in the group. If you're out of the group, you have to go to counseling, is that right?

Martha: No, you go to another building. You are kind of expelled from the colony. You've got to make your own campfire and cook your own meals over it, and it's pretty basic.

M: Pretty basic circumstances?

Martha: Pretty basic, yeah.

M: Okay. And when you said following through, Colin, what is that about?

Colin: Well it's like taking direction positively. Accepting what I have to do.

M: Taking direction, accepting what you have to do?

Colin: Mmm.

M: And you said taking space when you needed it. What do you mean by that?

Colin: Before when I was angry I'd start going around rampaging, just breaking things. But now I just stop and go out on the deck or just go out in the soccer field.

M: So you'd go around breaking things, and now you take time out?

Colin: Yep.

M: You go down on the deck or you go into the field. What is the deck?

Colin: Well there's like, it's the front part of the extension. Which is like a big building where we eat.

M: Is there anything else that you could tell me about taking space when you need it that would help me understand that? You said that . . .

Colin: Like I would . . . just depends what season it is. If it was winter, I'd go outside and I'd make, like, I'd roll the snow and make a snowman. I'd make snowballs and turn them into a snowman. If it was fall, I'd go outside and rake leaves.

M: So, it's . . .

Colin: Stuff that'll keep me busy.

M: Stuff that would keep you busy.

Colin: In a positive way.

M: In a positive way. And keeping busy in a positive way instead of what? Like you said, breaking things?

Colin: Instead of a negative way, right. I used to go around breaking windows.

M: Sorry?

Colin: Before, I used to go around breaking windows when I was angry.

M: Breaking noodles?

Colin: Windows!

M: Oh, I thought you said noodles; I'm sorry (laughter). It takes me a while to catch up with your accent. Breaking windows. Is there anything else that you could catch me up on about what you've noticed in your own life developing since August? You've talked about following through, taking space when you need it, staying in group. Anything else that you could catch me up on? Other developments that you've noticed?

Colin: I've just been happy and wanting to get that goal that I have planned finished.

M: And that goal is?

Colin: To get home.

M: To get home. What's made all this possible since August? Is it like your mom said, having an apartment to stay in?

Martha: I think there was something else too. I think it was that when behavior gets bad enough, criminal charges are laid, and he ended up in a youth secure detention facility, which is about the highest level of detainment...that you can reach for kids. And he was in there for 6 weeks, and it was a Christian organization. And I think they did a lot of good work with him.

M: Did they? Is that your sense as well? Do you know what your mom's talking about in terms of them doing good work with you?

Colin: Yeah, they helped me out.

M: How did they do that Colin? What did they do that worked for you?

Colin: They just did their job. Made sure we were all safe at all times.

M: Made sure that you were safe?

Colin: Made sure that everyone was safe? There, yeah.

M: Okay. And can I just come back to asking about a couple of these developments? You've mentioned "following through," "listening and taking direction," "accepting what you have to do." You talked about "taking space when you need it." So that, you know, previously you might be just caught up in breaking something, but now you're able to, what, walk away from that?

Colin: Yeah.

M: You also talked about "staying in group." Now, do you see these as positive developments in your life?

Colin: Yep.

M: Or are they just to do with you doing what you have to do to get out of this place. To get away from the detention center and back home as soon as you can?

Colin: A bit of both.

M: Bit of both. So these are things that you have to do to get away from the detention center, but they're also positive developments for you?

Colin: Yeah.

M: You are able to take space when you need it now, whereas before you were caught up in breaking something, or whatever. Now you can take time out, you can go to the deck or the field and make a snowman, or snow woman, rake leaves. What's your understanding about why that's positive in terms of your own development?

Colin: Because it's better for me to stay active if I'm angry. It's better for me to stay active when I'm angry. If not, I just shut down.

M: Sorry?

Colin: It's better for me to stay active when I'm angry in a positive way, and if I don't stay active I shut down.

M: Okay. It means that you don't shut down. Is that right?

Colin: Yeah.

M: So you have an idea that this development is a good development for your life?

Colin: Mmm.

M: Why is that? I mean, what's your sense of why this is a good development?

Colin: It's good because then I'll know in the future, if something really went wrong in the future, I'll know what I can do and how I'll do it.

M: So if something goes wrong you've got an ability to what, make changes, or...

Colin: Yeah.

M: Are you saying it's giving you a better future, or...

Colin: Yeah.

M: Okay, it gives you a better future and it gives you the ability to what, make changes? How would you say it?

Colin: Make changes.

M: Make changes? That works for you? Okay. And that fits with how you want your life to be. You want to be the sort of person who can make changes, who can have an effect on his own future? Is that right? Does that fit for you?

Colin: Yeah.

M: Have you always had that hope that you'd be able to be the sort of the person who could affect the course of his own future? Or is that a new idea for you?

Colin: It might not be a new idea, but I think it is. But I've always wanted to be able to do it.

M: You've always wanted to have this ability?

Colin: Yeah.

M: To change the course of your future. What would you call that sort *of step? Like you said, now you can take space when you need it. Now you know how to do that in a way that keeps you active. It's not just that you take space, it's also that you make sure that you act so you don't close things down, is that right?

Colin: Mmm.

M: So it's a double thing for you.

Colin: Yeah.

M: And this means that you've got more to say about your own future. What would you call that sort of development? Can you think of a name for it? Do you mind if I ask your mom?

Colin: Okay.

M: What sort of development would you say this is? How would you name this sort of development? You see your son being able to take time out but at the same time stay active, not shutting down, and have an effect on his future. What name . . .

Martha: Self-control.

M: Self-control. Okay, self-control. Does that fit for you Colin? Your mom said it was a development in self-control?

Colin: Yep. That's it.

M: Okay, self-control. It's good to find out a bit more about the steps that Colin's taking. I also want to find out a bit more about your steps too, because you've stayed in there and you've worked at it and you've recently obtained an apartment after a lot of frustration I understand.

Martha: That's so.

M: Let's just look back at these things, Colin. You talked about following through on things, listening, taking direction, and accepting what you have to do. And your mom said it was about the development of self-control. How's this affecting your life? What are you able to do now?

Colin: Well, it keeps putting me in a better position to move around, to make the changes that I need to be making.

M: It gives you a better position to move around, did you say?

Colin: Yes.

M: And it's a better position to make the changes that you need to be making, or the changes that you want to make?

Colin: Both, because I need to and want to.

M: Both. Okay. What's your sense about this? Would you say that's also a positive development, or would you say . . .

Colin: Yep.

M: You would say it's positive. How do you feel about this development when you think about being in a better position to move around and change what you need to change?

Colin: It's like a movie, or something. I'll know what I can expect might happen.

M: You'll know what you can expect?

Colin: Mm hm.

M: Say a bit more about that, about the reason that you feel positively about how you can know what to expect. Say a bit more about what you mean by that.

Colin: I'll know what might happen and I'll know what I need to do about this and how that's going to go.

M: What would you think about why that would be a positive development in Colin's, to follow through and be in a better position to move around and change what he needed and wanted to change? Do you know why that's something that's appealing to him?

Martha: Well everybody is entitled to that.

M: Entitled to?

Martha: That's like personal freedom, and everyone's entitled to it.

M: Oh.

Martha: I don't think that everybody is always given the same degree of opportunity in that department. He certainly wasn't.

M: That helps me understand. So, your mom said that she thought one of the reasons that this was a positive development for you is that it gave you personal freedom and that's something that you're entitled to. Does that strike a chord for you, what your mom said?

Colin: Yeah.

M: It does. What strikes a chord for you about that?

Colin: I didn't get the freedom that I needed, that I should've had when I was younger.

M: You didn't get the freedom that you needed to have when you were younger? What got in the way of that?

Colin: Just the man I was with. The man that my mom was with.

M: The man that your mom was living with? So, he took that freedom from you?

Colin: (nods).

Scaffolding Conversations

At this point in the therapeutic conversation, it was my understanding that we had all traveled a considerable distance in a relatively brief period of time. The point of entry to this conversation was Colin's action in walking out on the deck when frustrated. This was a development that had been particularly noticed by the regular therapist, Judy, who thought this might provide a point of entry for the development of an alternative storyline. When I initially consulted Martha and Colin about this action, Martha was of the opinion that this had already been talked about and that there was nothing more to discuss about it. However, both Martha and Colin were willing to respond to my questions about this initiative. In the context of the therapeutic inquiry that I then initiated, it turned out that there was a lot more to say about "walking out on the deck." This initiative became vastly significant. It became saturated with meaning and was rendered symbolic. It symbolized both Colin's aspiration to affect the course of his future and what he held precious in life, that is, freedom. He'd not previously given voice to this aspiration, or emphasized, in this way, the value he accorded to freedom.

In his expressions of this aspiration and of what he accorded value to, Colin had separated from aspects of the known and familiar about his life—that he was a young man who was a concrete thinker and who was incapable of reflecting on his life—and had begun to approach what might be possible for him to know about his life. The expressions of this aspiration to affect the course of his future, and this account of the value he gives to freedom, constitute intentional understandings of his life and understandings of what he holds precious, and these represent principles of living that are abstractions. I believe that these developments in Colin's capacity to reflect on his own life and to think about his life in abstract terms are, in part, the outcome of a therapeutic conversation in which careful attention had been given to the scaffolding of the zone of proximal development—that zone of learning between the known and familiar and the possible to know. This scaffolding facilitated an incremental and progressive distancing from the known and familiar toward what it is possible for Colin to know and to do.

Categories of Learning Tasks

Influenced by the ideas of Vygotsky, I have developed a "scaffolding conversations" map that is structured by five categories of inquiry. This map can be utilized to provide a guide to the development of therapeutic conversations that facilitate incremental and progressive movements across the proximal zone of learning. The categories of inquiry on this map establish specific learning tasks, which I define as the following:

1. Low-level distancing tasks; that is, tasks that encourage people to characterize specific objects and events of their worlds
2. Medium-level distancing tasks; that is, tasks that encourage people to bring into relationship specific objects and events of their world in the development of chains of association, or "complexes," that establish bonds and relations between these objects and events
3. Medium-high–level distancing tasks; that is, tasks that encourage people to reflect on these chains of association and to draw, from these, realizations and learnings about specific phenomena
4. High-level distancing tasks; that is, tasks that encourage people to abstract these realizations and learnings from their concrete and specific circumstances in the formation of concepts about life and identity
5. Very-high–level distancing tasks; that is, tasks that encourage the formulation of predictions about the outcome of specific

actions founded on this concept development, and tasks that encourage the planning for, and initiation of, such actions

Colin's expressions of, and aspiration to affect, the course of his own future, and of the extent to which he held freedom precious, are intentional understandings about his life, and understandings of what he accords value to in life, that provide the foundations of concept development. In the context of extended therapeutic conversations, the word meaning of these understandings can be developed and redeveloped to the point that these achieve the status of concepts about life and identity. This, in turn, provides a foundation for people to proceed to address the predicaments of their lives and to more significantly influence the shape of their existence.

From the Known and Familiar to What Is Possible to Know

Low-Level Distancing Tasks

Low-level distancing tasks are tasks that encourage people to characterize specific objects and events of their worlds.

In the early part of this conversation, I invited Colin and Martha to characterize the initiative that Colin had taken in going onto the deck. At this time, the initiative was defined as "taking space when I need it." A number of associated developments were also named, including "staying in group," "following through," and "self-control." I then asked for further clarification of these descriptions and, in response to this, "following through" was further defined as "taking direction positively" and "accepting what I have to do."

Medium-Level Distancing Tasks

Medium-level distancing tasks are tasks that encourage people to bring into relationship specific objects and events of their world in the development of chains of association, or "complexes," that establish bonds and relations between these objects and events.

In response to my inquiry into the consequences of these initiatives that had now been firmly characterized, I learned that these had made it possible for Colin to be "like everyone else," "to get special privileges, like going to the movies," to avoid actions that might precipitate negative consequences" and to instead "roll the snow and make a snowman," to "keep busy in a positive way," and "to get home." Later I also learned that these developments were putting Colin "in a better position to move around, to make the changes that I need to be making."

Medium-High–Level Distancing Tasks

Medium-high–level distancing tasks are tasks that encourage people to reflect on these chains of associations and to draw, from these, realizations and learnings about specific phenomena.

On interviewing Colin about his reflections on these developments, I learned that he judged them to be positive in the sense that these would assist him to leave the detention center and would place him in a position in which he would know "what I can expect might happen" and in which he would "know what I need to do about this."

High-Level Distancing Tasks

High-level distancing tasks are tasks that encourage people to abstract these realizations and learnings from their concrete and specific circumstances in the formation of concepts about life and identity.

On consulting Colin and Martha about why they might judge these developments to be positive, and about why these realizations about how Colin could know what to expect and know what he needed to do were important, Colin gave voice to an aspiration to affect the course of his future, and Martha and Colin gave voice to what is precious him, and to what he is entitled to—"freedom." These intentional understandings about Colin's life, and these understandings about what he gives value to, represent the beginnings of the formation of concepts about life and identity.

Very-High–Level Distancing Tasks

Very-high–level distancing tasks are tasks that encourage the formulation of predictions about the outcome of a specific actions founded on this concept development, and tasks that encourage the planning for and initiation of such actions.

This interview occurred in a workshop context, which included a post-session discussion with the workshop participants. In the context of this post-session discussion, Colin defined a couple of steps that he had a sense of being ready to take and that were in harmony with the realizations that he had given voice to in the therapeutic conversation, and with what he had become familiar with in terms of his intentional understandings about his life and with the understandings of what he accorded value to in life.

Returning to Colin and Martha

In speaking about the family context in which a man that Martha had been living with had taken Colin's freedom when he was young, Martha spoke strongly of her sense of complicity in what Colin had been subject to by this man. Martha reflected that she could have been immobilized by guilt on account of this. On hearing this declaration, I interviewed her about developments in her life that had made it possible for her to escape this guilt that could have been so immobilizing. In response to this, Martha described a recent turning point in her life. Three years earlier she'd had a mental health crisis and had been diagnosed with major depression. She said that until this time she'd always assumed that all of the difficulties of her life had to do with the fact that "I wasn't trying hard enough." Following this diagnosis, Martha developed a firm resolve that "nothing that had happened in the past was going to stop me now."

M: So that was a turning point, and then you had this realization "nothing's going to stop me now."

Martha: That's right.

M: Is that a sentiment that you've had before in your life: "Nothing's going to stop me now?" Or was that a new sentiment to have about life?

Martha: It's a new one.

M: So, this helped you to step into this new sentiment "Nothing's going to stop me now."

Martha: That's right.

M: What does that sentiment fit with? Did it fit with certain hopes or dreams that you had for your own life? Or...

Martha: Yes, because now I could execute what I intended to do without this interference that I could not understand but kept blaming myself for.

M: So it made it possible to execute those intentions?

Martha: Right.

M: Those intentions had been there for a long time, it's just that you weren't free to execute them?

Martha: I didn't feel free to execute them, and when people would say to me, "It's just a matter of choice," as is often told to the kids at the detention center, and that is true to an extent, but some people's amount of control over the choice thing isn't all equal.

M: What were those intentions that you really always wanted to execute but it wasn't possible for you to? What were those intentions that you always wanted to get behind?

Martha: Well, to be a good mother, to be a good citizen, to be myself.

M: And those intentions go way back for you? Did you have those intentions even when you were quite young?

Martha: Yeah.

M: Were these the sorts of intentions that were shared by other members of your family?

Martha: No.

M: They weren't? Were they uniquely your own intentions?

Martha: Yes.

M: They wouldn't have matched the intentions of other family members?

Martha: No.

M: And you can remember having these intentions for you life when you were quite young?

Martha: Yes, well, the mother part wasn't...

M: Which parts were there when you were quite young? You talked about your intentions to be a good mother, a good citizen, being yourself, and...

Martha: Being myself, and just, you know, doing pleasurable things, and feeling good and happiness.... It was very difficult for me. I guess it is for lots of people.

M: So it had to do with your intentions. To feel good, for happiness. And it had to do with certain hopes that you had for your life?

Martha: Yeah. And my life was very, very controlled.

M: Controlled.

Martha: I lived with two grandparents. She was the matriarch, and half of them were Catholic and half of them were Protestant, and they were more concerned about how my soul was going to go to hell if I was with this one or that one than they were about if I ever got to heaven! You know what I mean? It was a nightmare.

M: It was a nightmare.

Martha: Yes.

M: This helps me understand just how different your intentions were. There was this nightmare on the one side, "is your soul going to hell," but on the other side you have these hopes for pleasurable things, for feeling good, for happiness, for a different life, and these were not the same as the intentions of other people in the family.

Martha: No, and they wanted to make me into a lady because we lived in a kind of, I don't know, upper middle-class area. We had to wear white gloves and hats and, oh my goodness, it was awful.

M: Did these intentions also fit with what Colin is saying about freedom. About, you know, stepping into more freedom?

Martha: I suppose so.

M: That's a theme for you and for Colin? Stepping into more freedom? Is it reasonable to understand it that way?

Martha: Yeah, yeah.

M: How did you manage to keep all of those hopes and intentions alive for all of that time? For pleasurable things, for feeling good, for happiness and hope? For the freedom? How did you manage to hold onto all of that, because it was so different to the people around you?

Martha: Good walls.

M: Good walls, good walls around you? You knew how to do that?

Martha: I built them.

M: You built some good walls?

Martha: Yeah.

Discussion I

Tom: Michael wants us to speak.

Harlene: I think so, yeah. So my first comment is that I think he's very clear about his ideas about people's potential, very clear about his goal as a therapist and very clear about the skill sets needed to reach that goal.

Tom: And what are your thoughts about that?

Harlene: My thoughts are that he does a very good job of articulating his work, the ideas or the scaffold that supports his work. One of the things I was very curious about during the interview was his inner talk. What was the conversation going on in his head as he was asking the questions and making the comments?

Jaakko: There are a lot of interesting pieces in Michael's interview. Having these dialogical glasses as I have, it was very interesting to hear him so clearly say, "It's not my task to give positive connotations or reframing to the things." I like that very much—"It's my task to become involved in their lives." This was very dialogical conversation in many ways, not least in the sense that he was so careful to take in the words of the clients and continue the story. I liked that very much. What happens in my mind as happened here was, when you do what Michael did here, the time stops. Perhaps that's not the accurate way to put it, but at least it slows down. We go from second to second or a half second to the next one, and that, in my mind, is the place where Colin got more and more possibilities for the use of his own resources.

Tom: Michael spoke about initiatives, survival of important initiatives, and from there he used the word *platform* and then the word *scaffold*. Then he changed the word *scaffold* to *scaffolder* and even more active, *scaffolding*. Then he spoke of *scaffolding skills*. What is Michael doing in his scaffoldings? He was making notes very eagerly and he spoke out loud, what he wrote down. So I thought that could be one way of his scaffolding, writing things down and reading them out loud.

Jaakko: Perhaps that is also a way to slow down the time, making those notes.

Tom: Yeah. So what does this man do when he's scaffolding? This conversation reminds me of a man I met in my last year in medical school. He was a radiologist, working with X-rays. He should demonstrate a picture of the chest to see the shadow of the heart. He said, "I never start to look first at what I'm asked to look for. I go to the periphery first, I look at the ribs." I had that image of Michael scaffolding, looking out there to see possibilities, not focusing so much straight on, but looking out.

Jaakko: I've got a pretty big question in my mind, actually. I'm very curious to see what will happen with it later. The question is, "Where do we need Michael's explanation of what has taken place? What is the place of this construction of the scaffolds in the theory?" The reason I have this question is because I have become very careful or even a little bit afraid of theories. They are needed, but how do we use them? That's the place where we become power users. Coming into theories is always a shift from this relation that takes place in a situation. Theories give us the power to define and use. I'm very curious to see what happens with this theory later.

Tom: I would use a stronger word. I'm also a bit concerned, when he started the scaffolder, scaffolding, and then suddenly scaffolding skills. Where are those skills? One can easily think it's inside the person, the scaffolder. In the very end, he talked about intention. That's also interesting. That's not a relational word.

Harlene: So I'm still curious about what was going on in his inner talk, as he was talking. What was he saying to himself in terms of what he was trying to do?

Jaakko: I have to repeat what I said, although I'm a little bit afraid of theories, we need them all the time.

Tom: Do we?

Jaakko: We do. You too.

Tom: No. Theory comes from the Greek word *theorem*. That means "to see." You cannot see the invisible world; you have to do something else.

Jaakko: Yeah, I see your point, yeah.

Tom: I really hope Michael himself will point out on the interview and say, "This is my scaffolding principles or my scaffolding theories."

Jaakko: Do you want to comment on this, Michael?

Michael: Yes. I want to go back to the question of where these skills are. One constructivist position is that everything is constructed in language, and that we only have constructions. My own approach is more Foucaultian. I've been very influenced by the ideas of Michel Foucault. He argues that constructions of knowledge are always associated with practices of living, and the two are not the same. These constructions and practices are in a relationship of mutual dependency, but they are not one and the same thing. There are constructs of the world and there are practices of living—practices of the self and practices of relationship—which are intimately linked to those constructs. These practices of living can be considered to be skills of self-formation and relationship-formation, many of which, according to Foucault, are practices of power. At times Foucault is misrepresented on this: "Foucault said that power is knowledge" or "Foucault exposed knowledge as power." He in fact strongly rejected this sort of formulation, insisting that power and knowledge are distinct.

According to this understanding, we, as therapists, have our constructions of therapeutic practice, but our work is also shaped by specific practices that are intimately linked to these constructs, and these practices can be regarded as skills.

Tom: So practice scaffolding?

Michael: I believe that the scaffolding of therapeutic conversations is a skill, one that can always be further developed. But, more than this, I believe that all therapeutic conversations are shaped by specific practices or skills, regardless of the orientation of the therapist. Therapists are not simply engaging with constructs of therapeutic practice.

Tom: May I say two words about *construct,* which has been a big word in the field? And *create* was a big word for a while. And both words have Latin roots. At the moment, I prefer the word *generate.* That word has a Greek root, meaning "people to be born," "things to be produced," or "events to take place." A construct could easily be an individual thing, going back to constructive or creative. I believe everything is flowing through us, through generations. So I prefer the word *generate* at the moment.

Jaakko: Michael, you said skills don't belong to the world of constructs. Was that the point you made, or ... ?

Michael: No, I was observing that constructs and practices go together, but that they are distinct. They're together and require each other. I believe that we all have constructions of therapeutic conversations, that these constructions are tied to specific practices, and that these practices can be likened to skills. Tom, you said "*intentional* is not a relational word," but "relating" is not just something that is generated in the moment between people. It is generally accepted that our constructs of life and identity have a social and cultural history. And what I am proposing is that what we refer to as relational is in fact a "relational style" that also has a social and cultural history, and that it is in the context of this social and cultural history that some relational styles are valued over other relational styles.

For example, in regard to therapeutic practice, in the 1970s, there was the development of the "personal growth" therapies, and associated with these therapies was a particular relational style or relational practice, which was quite distinct and included relatively intense "eye-to-eye" contact, specific practices of the body, such as upright posture, open face, one's arms and legs uncrossed, palms resting on one's lap, face up, a particular modulation of the voice, and so on. This relational style was explicitly coached and therefore explicitly evident, but I believe that all constructions of therapeutic practice are associated with relational style, even if therapists are hesitant to acknowledge this.

I am personally very interested in this consideration and believe that transparency of relational style is vital to the further development of therapeutic practice, to skills development. But I don't know if this is interesting to anyone else.

Harlene: Yes, it is. So, Michael, back to trying to help me understand something. I'm just curious, because you were giving your "after" descriptions of medium-high–level distancing questions, medium-level distancing questions, and so on. To help me and maybe others, when you were in the conversation with the family, and you're asking your questions and participating in the conversations, what's your inner talk? Are you thinking in terms of categories of questions, or is your practice so spontaneous for you now that you don't have those thoughts and they are more like after descriptions?

Michael: It is my experience that I am improvisational in my therapeutic conversations. I experience spontaneity in these conversations. I don't have a question prepared ahead of hearing a person's response to my last question. But I don't see any contradiction between spontaneity and rigor in therapeutic practice, or between improvisation and the meticulous attention to the development of therapeutic skills. And I don't perceive a contradiction between what I have said about therapeutic style and improvisation.

At times, music metaphors have been employed to characterize therapeutic practice. I like these metaphors. I'm very fond of live jazz, and at times find myself in awe of skilled and creative improvisation. Now, skilled and creative improvisation is founded on practice, practice, and more practice. These musicians have engaged in a rigor of practice, have been meticulous in the development of skills. And no amount of practice is too much practice for these musicians. And in regard to these reflections on style, style in clearly evident in this skilled and creative improvisation. This style can always be discerned. This is clearly not rock and roll, swing, or blues.

So, I believe that whenever we can say about our work and life, "Well, I feel very spontaneous in this," there can be found a history of practice in this domain of expression. This history of practice is profoundly significant in terms of how we respond to the particularities of the moment, in terms of the repertoire of responses available to us in our therapeutic conversations.

Jaakko: Would you mind calling this a dialogical practice, what you did with the family in this consultation?

Michael: It is dialogical, but anything dialogical is also cultural and historical.

Tom: One question still concerning the interview. You said he has a big shift, a big change. Can you say what you saw or heard that made you think this is a big step?

Michael: I believe there were several significant shifts. First, Colin, a young man considered unable to foresee the consequences of his actions, brings some initiatives into relationship with specific consequences and conditions in the building of chains of association. Foreseeing the consequences of one's actions is founded on the development of this sort of complex thinking. Then, Colin, with my assistance and with the assistance of his mother, gives voice to specific intentional understandings about his life and to understandings about what he gives value to. These understandings represent the development of abstract thought and create fertile conditions for the sort of concept development that provides people with a foundation to intervene in the shaping of their own lives.

I believe that another significant shift is evident in the identification of the history of what it is that Martha has wanted for her life as a woman and a mother but hadn't experienced the "freedom to execute." Again, what is evident here is the development and rich description of specific intentional understandings of life and of understandings of what Martha gives value to in life. It was my hope that the further development of this avenue of inquiry would render visible the social and relational history of what both Colin and Martha intend for their lives and of what they both give value to. Further, it was my hope that they both might experience the stories of their lives to be linked around these themes. However, at this point we were facing a cul-de-sac, as Martha had provided a psychological account of the survival of what it was that she held precious. Although this psychological explanation is clearly positive, it is nonetheless "thin" and a roadblock to rich story development and to the social and relational history of what she holds precious. In response, I sought an avenue beyond this cul-de-sac by asking Martha about who might have verified these other hopes for her life.

The Interview (continuing)

M: Did anybody ever validate these other hopes for your life? Was there anyone around that would have shared these hopes for your life?

Martha: Yes.

M: Who would that be?

Martha: Umm... The one grandmother, but she died of heart disease.

M: One grandmother. How do you know that she would have validated these hopes for you?

Martha: I could feel that.

M: You could feel it. What was her name?

Martha: Hilda.

M: Grandmother Hilda. What could you feel from her?

Martha: Love.

M: Love. And she died when you were quite young?

Martha: Yeah.

M: How old were you at the time?

Martha: Umm... At 10, I was sent to live with my father because she was dying and he, my father, would not sign the paperwork to allow me to go with her to Arizona where she was retiring.

M: Oh...

Martha: That was a battle. I was very much treated like a possession in my life. So I separated from her then, but she actually died when I was 14.

M: And she would have never treated you like a possession.

Martha: No, it was very different.

M: And you experienced love from her?

Martha: Yes.

M: Do you know what it was that she appreciated about you?

Martha: Me. That I was unique in my own way.

M: Because you're unique in your own way. Do you know what it was about the "me" that she appreciated so much?

Martha: Umm... She knew that I had deep feelings. I was a touchy-feely person (laugh).

M: She appreciated the fact that you had deep feelings and that you were a touchy-feely person.

Martha: Yeah.

M: What does that mean, touchy-feeling person? That you were what, sensitive, or...

Martha: Well, as opposed to someone who was more intellectual and doesn't show their feelings,

M: Expressive with feelings?

Martha: Right, or than a more practical person.

M: So she really appreciated that in you. That you were a touchy-feely person, that you are expressive with your feelings?

Martha: Yeah.

M: And she would have had also hopes that you had a pleasurable life and got to feel happy and to have freedom? She would have wanted this for you?

Martha: Yeah.

M: What would it be like if she could be here and listening to this conversation about how you'd now stepped into those intentions that you've held onto through all this time? What's your guess about how she'd be feeling for you?

Martha: She'd be happy, and happy for me too.

M: I can only imagine what it would be like for her to know that, even though you were split off from each other, you kept the spirit of that connection alive and the sorts of things that you were joined together in. . . . Actually I have a rather nice sense of your grandmother, as if she were here right now. It's quite lovely. I feel quite warmed up by this, so thank you for sharing this.

Martha: That's okay (smiling).

M: What I've just understood is that you'd held on to these intentions despite everything that you've been through. It's just that you weren't able to execute them. These included hopes around pleasurable things, for feeling good, for happiness and for freedom, as well as being the sort of mother that you wanted to be. And your grandmother Hilda actually acknowledged this and you felt joined with her in these intentions and hopes.

Martha: Mmm hmm. That's it.

M: And that she appreciated your touchy-feeling, deep expressiveness. And that she'd feel quite joyful about you arriving at this point?

Martha: Yes. Yes.

M: How's this conversation going for you, Colin?

Colin: Good.

M: Is it? Why do you say it's good, Colin, what . . .

Colin: Because I'm understanding a bit about everything, and . . .

M: What are you understanding that's important to you?

Colin: What I've been learning about myself, and what I've been learning about things have been going.

M: Understanding about yourself and about how things have been going?

Colin: Yeah.

M: You've been listening to me having a conversation with your mom about how she's also stepping into freedom just like you are, and that it's been a long journey for her.

Colin: I think we have a lot of similarities.

M: A lot of similarities. So did you know about your Grandma Hilda?

Colin: (shakes head)

M: You didn't know about her? What's it like to hear about the fact that you had a grandmother, a grandma who...

Colin: Well I knew I had a grandma. I didn't know I had two grandmothers.

M: This is your great-grandma. Great-grandma Helen. What would she be appreciating about what Colin is doing? What would she be appreciating about what Colin's been achieving?

Martha: Because she had very little power assigned to her in that household, and it was assigned, believe me! And yet her small, almost behind the scenes or in spite of it, maneuvers, could carry through.

M: So in spite of the fact that...

Martha: And with more impact than anybody else who did a lot more blustering and control taking, and whatever.

M: So, just the fact that Helen had very little power, and yet, despite that, what she achieved could be carried through, with more impact than anyone would have imagined. This would be like a message to her that it was all worth something?

Martha: It was worth something, right!!

M: To see Colin stepping into freedom in these ways.

Martha: She took a lot of flack for standing up for me when I misbehaved.

M: Did she?

Martha: Oh yeah (laughs)!

M: How would she feel about what Colin's doing then? How would she feel toward him if she realized that this was an example of how, despite the fact that she had little power and freedom was taken from her, she had more impact on your life and the lives of others to come in the family than those who had all the control.

Martha: Proud.

M: She'd be proud of him?

Martha: Yes.

M: What is it that she would have been proud of?

Martha: Umm...That's [pause]. She too was very guilt-ridden, and she would have been relieved for her personal self and, you know, proud to see the results of something that she kept at, you know.

M: Proud to see the results of something that she kept at!

Martha: Yeah.

M: That's beautiful. What is it like for you to hear that, Colin? Does this interest you or does it not interest you?

Colin: Yeah, I'm really interested, because I never knew my great-grandmother, and that she would have been proud of me, and that she and my mother and I have similarities. Like she was there for my mother and my mother's there for me.

M: What does it mean to you that your great-grandmother would be proud of you?

Colin: It means that I had someone who could have looked forward to being with me, and just knowing that she'd be happy with this.

M: Colin, I've been hearing about a lot of developments in your life: following through, taking space when you need it, not just taking space but staying active so that you don't shut down, having more impact on your own future, stepping into freedom that was taken from you, and so on. What sort of direction in life is this?

Colin: A positive direction.

M: Positive direction? Would there be any other names? Like, if this was a new trail in your life, or pathway, what would you call it?

Colin: Succeed to going home. It's going pretty well compared with the difficulties in my past...

This excerpt of the transcript of my conversation with Martha and Colin gives an account of the distance that can be traveled in one therapeutic conversation from the starting point of a unique outcome. At the end of this conversation, we were a long way from the starting point, which was Colin's act of walking onto the deck of the cafeteria of the detention center. By the end of this interview, this act had become highly symbolic. It had become symbolic of a theme of freedom around which Colin's life was linked to his mother's life and to his great-grandmother's life. This linking of the stories of people's lives around shared themes contributes to rich story development. In this rich story development the intentional understandings, and the understandings about what people give value to are developed and redeveloped, and become generalized themes about life and identity. This provides a foundation for people to proceed with their lives, for, in this development, a range of options for actions that would be coherent with these themes become more visible and available.

Discussion II

Harlene: I have much respect for the care and vigor that you put into thinking about your work and trying to describe it. I think that's often something that's missing in clinicians' work. We often work so automatically and we don't give enough care and consideration; we're not rigorous enough in terms of how we think about work, in terms of the words we use to describe it or explain it.

Tom: Would you prefer us to talk to you, or to talk among ourselves so you can be free to . . .

Michael: I'll sit out and listen to you talk among yourselves.

Tom: So you can let your mind go? Where?

Michael: What are the options? Exotic locations?

Harlene: Spain?

Tom: Iraq? Did you mean . . . you said it's so much lacking in much work?

Harlene: I said that Michael puts so much rigor into thinking about his work and describing it and attaching it to theoretical constructs. A lot of therapists, of course, don't do that. They just operate on automatic pilot and are not very self-reflective or do not do much critical analysis of their work.

Tom: So he's bending back on himself.

Harlene: I think so, yes.

Jaakko: What strikes me all the time is that this story was so lovely. I try to look at it through these dialogical glasses and I felt that I was so near to what was taken place. I was happy about many of the questions and points that were made, because I could easily have described it also with different theoretical formulations. It seems there are a lot of possibilities for us to put this into a theoretical frame. I, of course, have nothing against the theoretical frame, which Michael has for his work, because I think that theoretical frames are something that is fitting for our ways of being in this. The idea that it was so polyphonic and especially taking more of the voice or the voices of the great-grandmother, who became a resource in the consultation.... As I already said, it continued to be very dialogical, taking into account that all of them in the room could follow all the time and they were not left out.

Harlene: I was thinking about not only what was said out loud, but my guess is that there was a lot of inner talk for the boy and the mother. I'm also curious about what the referring therapist was thinking and what difference it makes for her, and I'm sure that Michael will give us some information on that later on.

Tom: In the beginning, he was very much occupied with the word *practice,* or *practicing.* If somebody should ask me what Michael does, what is his practice, I would highlight his strong, warm presence. What I also noticed was that sometimes, I think even several times when they said something and they came up with a concept, he said, "What does it mean?" He is very active in finding the meaning of the words. And one thing I wondered about was, "What did Michael think of the laughter of Martha?" What did you think of her laughter?

Jaakko: I was thinking perhaps the same thing, the laughter, and I was supposing that for a therapist or a consultant sitting in that kind of situation, you could put it into the open in many ways and I suppose there was a lot of inner talk in Michael, "How should I deal with it? Should I comment on it or..."

Tom: "Let it go?"

Jaakko: Yeah.

Harlene: I was thinking about your mention of Michael's presence and bringing up the inner talk, which goes back to what I was struggling with earlier. Obviously Michael does have a strong presence in the therapy room. I asked him, "What is your inner talk? How do you make your choices?" Because I was imagining that people are thinking, "How can I do this if I wanted to start doing scaffolding, so to speak, in my practice? And how do you know what part of it is Michael himself?" I think that's difficult, you see someone doing something and you want to do it. It looks energizing, useful, it looks like successful therapy, and I want to add this to my practice. But you can't go around being a little Michael. You can't duplicate Michael.

Tom: Yes, I will!

Harlene: I'm going to tell Bush (then U.S. president) that.

Jaakko: What would be most difficult is the Australian accent.

(Reflectors and audience laughing)

Tom: And Bush will speak with Howard (then prime minister of Australia)?

Harlene: Yeah. But making sense of what I'm struggling with, in other words, how do you grasp a concept or the conceptual aspect of someone's work, the practice of it, and be able to do it yourself and use it yourself in your own style? That's the asset of each of us, our own style, each of us meaning everyone in this room, not just us.

Tom: Sure. I think I'm much slower in the room with people than outside the room. I'm much, much less talkative in the room than being with friends, like the two of you.

Harlene: I wonder what Michael's thinking.

Jaakko: I want to add something. Because last time, just 3 years ago, that we met Michael, and I can't remember all the tapes we saw, but of course the basic tunes of being present in the meeting were very similar. Perhaps we can speak of how the style is, but style again is a kind of term that is, if not frozen, it puts frames.

Harlene: Not a good word, but for lack of a better term.

Jaakko: I know what you're saying. But I also saw differences to what I saw 3 years ago. I very much liked one question, I can't remember what the point was, but Colin said something like, "It's important to do this and this." He said it's very important to do this. Michael didn't take it for granted; he asked, "Why is it so important?" And it opened up a way to go further along. So it's a way to take away our pre-assumptions as much as possible.

Michael: I'll join you now. I enjoyed listening to those reflections, and it would be nice to have more time for our conversation to develop. I was thinking about what Tom said about bending back on oneself. It is not a metaphor that I've had in my mind, but it seems just so appropriate. I wanted to ask you more about that metaphor. What does it mean to you?

Tom: Well, actually the word *reflect* means to bend back.

Michael: So how did you see/hear me bending back on myself?

Tom: Well, as Harlene said, you are constantly re-thinking what you have experienced and make change of it and find words, and shift the words and new words... It seems you are thinking and re-thinking all the time.

Michael: It seems an appropriate metaphor. Bending backward is the thinking and the re-thinking of everything that's going on. In my mind, this metaphor represents therapy as a form of gymnastics. I can relate to this, as everybody gets a good workout in a therapeutic conversation.

Jaakko, you were talking about not accepting anything as given, and you gave some examples. Would you reflect more on this? You talked about how, on occasions, during my conversation with Colin and Martha, I'd request clarifications: "I don't understand. Why do you think that's a good development?" Could you talk more about the importance that you give to these requests for clarification?

Jaakko: Yes, of course. I'm a strange guy myself, because I learn most of my mistakes and I realize...

Michael: I didn't say that you were a strange guy. Tom told me this. (Laughing)

Jaakko (laughing): You knew it before! Okay. I think there is a very important situation where the client has thought that I did wrong, when I continued with a very simple idea how I thought life would be. In one consultation, it happened in Hamburg this winter, and we were meeting with a family, a special kind of family with a son being about 30 years of age and having a very difficult psychotic episode, manic behavior. It was a family of a quite successful business, and he almost ruined the enterprise they were running. His sister, who has moved from Canada to Germany to help her brother, said, "I'm so desperate that I can't help my brother. He's such a big part of my life." And I asked, "How big a part is he? Could you say a percentage, 100 or 0?" She said, "It's 60 percent." And I thought, "Wow, that's a lot." I was going to say it sounds like a lot, but then I realized I have to ask it. "Is it good, this way, or should it be less or more?" She said it should be much more. It was very surprising to me, but I was fortunate to not give my normalizing idea how I would see that we have to be independent and take care of our lives and so on. In those kinds of situations, I always have this in my mind. Not to take anything as a given but always to be open to discussions.

Michael: I am drawn to your comment about the hazards of normalizing ideas. In the culture of the professional disciplines, there is a lot of encouragement for us to subject people to these normalizing ideas: "So, this problem is splitting you off from the family. This must be terrible"; "I understand that this situation is depriving you of a formal education. This must be very upsetting to you"; "I can see that you are not being very productive in these efforts. To find yourself in this position is obviously very difficult for you." In standing back from these normalizing ideas, we are able to ask questions that open up important conversations: "Do you mind being split off from the family, and, if so, why do you mind this?" "What's it like for you to be separating from a formal education? If this is an issue for you, what could you tell me that would help me understand why this is so?"

"You said that you have come to a standstill in your efforts to achieve this. How is this experience for you?"

I'd also like to respond to what you said, Harlene, about being in a dialogue. One of the things I'm aware of in regard to the inner dialogue that you mentioned is that it gets richer in the course of many therapeutic conversations. Therapeutic conversations have the potential to re-invigorate this internal dialogue for all parties. This, in turn, is shaping of the therapist's responses and the responses of people who are seeking consultation. This is a phenomenon that I would like to explore more fully.

Harlene: I was asking you, because I know that it's difficult to pin-point and particularly in retrospect, when you're looking at your work after the fact. That's why I was thinking if there's a way to have a running, out-loud inner dialogue as you're having your other out-loud dialogue. To have more of a sense of what is going on in our heads and how to be aware of that. But I had the sense that you were being careful. You were active and asking lots of questions, but they weren't rapid fire. I think, as you or someone else mentioned, taking notes slows things down, giving you time to think before you pose your next question.

Michael: We are careful, because we have a position of significant responsibility for the outcome of these conversations, for the shaping effects of these conversations on people's sense of their lives and on their conclusions about their identities, and, of course, on their actions. The importance of observing this significant ethical responsibility for the effects of what we say and do in the name of therapy is a sentiment that I have also heard you and Tom and Jaakko expressing.

Tom: Would it be useful if we shared some words, what is going on in our inner talks during meetings?

Michael: What's the answer to that question?

Tom: Either "No, I don't think it's useful," or "I think that's useful."

Harlene: Or you can talk about it.

Tom: I will gladly share, but I don't want to impose it on you. I have a lot of interest for that talk, but I won't say it before you ask.

Michael: At times I invite people to ask me what has been occurring to me in the course of our therapeutic conversations. So this would be more directed by people's interest than by my assumptions about what it would be helpful for me to speak of.

Jaakko: Can I comment on this? I have a very peculiar way to deal with those inner ideas. I try to not put them open, but make sure that I have listened to every voice in my mind. And in a way, I try, in every meeting, to affect my way of being in the conversation. Some of them are ideas, which I put in the open, and some others are voices of my uneasiness of something. I try to put them in the open by saying, "I have a feeling that we have been discussing a lot of interesting and important issues, but there may perhaps still be things that we haven't spoken about." Speaking with my voice, that tells me that perhaps there is something that wasn't possible to say. So in this way, I try not to lead them to the open, but I let them affect what I'm doing in some way. Of course, it's not possible to do it every time with all the voices.

Harlene: I'm not struggling with if it's important to share your inner talk with the client or not. I'm asked this all the time and that's one of the reasons I'm asking Michael. People say, "Where did that question come from? Why did you comment on that? When someone said this, why didn't you say that?" For me, there is no answer to this question right now. But do we have any kind of awareness of what informs where we're coming from in any one moment?

Tom: I have often in the talk, which never comes out loud, said, "This is hard for you." And I say, "Don't be afraid. I should be here to protect you." I often say that. But I have to do that, for I'm trying to search for the painful part. I have to do that to protect them. But I never say it out loud.

Michael: In this presentation I have endeavored to be transparent about where I am coming from in my contribution to the therapeutic conversation. To this end I have shared some ideas about the scaffolding of these conversations, which influence my responses. I have referred to the ethical responsibility that

I have for the consequences of the way that I participate in
these conversations, and my efforts to be observant in regard
to this ethical responsibility influences my responses. I have
referred to the extent to which therapeutic style is also a
significant piece of where I am coming from, and have a
commitment to search out the way in which my responses
are being shaped by this style, so that I might be more con-
scious of the self and relationship-shaping activities that I
am sponsoring in the context of therapeutic conversations,
so that I might be more selective in regard to the therapeutic
skills that I want to further develop, and so that I might not
be so unwittingly reproducing whatever I might be reproducing that might be complicating to the lives of others
and that might contradict my chosen position on ethics and
on what I give value to. Then there is the awareness of the
hazards of sponsoring normative ideas about life, and this
awareness is a significant part of where we are coming from.
And I have referred to the extent to which many therapeutic
conversations contribute to the invigoration of inner experience for all parties to this conversation, which in turn significantly influences the development of the conversation
and shapes our responses to each other, which you might
refer to as the dialogical dimension. All of this is just part
of the story in response to Harlene's question about where I
am coming from in any one moment.

Jaakko: That was an interesting point because I started to think about
the opposite. Our practices are changing, and that has to do
with our inner dialogue changing. They are not separate. I
used to work in the beginning of my career with families
based on these systemic ideas, and I have so much fun thinking nowadays what kind of inner dialogue I had while doing
that, sitting with the families. It was all different than it is
now. How do we put our questions into the open? How do
we work? Because it's also in connection with what is taking
place in our inner dialogue, and they are on the same line.

Michael: So it's something about how we are orienting to the conversations, isn't it?

Jaakko: Yeah.

Harlene: And the word that we were talking about the first two days, *responsive* or being responsive to the other person or responding into the conversation.

Tom: The word *Martha's laughter* did not come from you. The word *laughter* came from this group. How was that to hear? I wondered what Michael thought of her laughter. How was that for you to hear? Was it inappropriate?

Michael: I don't have a sense of what's appropriate and what's not. There's a context to everything, so . . .

Tom: Was it out of context?

Michael: Of course it was in the context of Martha's experiences. But I can only guess about this context. There was an outsider-witness reflection at the end of my conversation with Martha and Colin. This was clearly a powerful experience for Martha, who responded by saying that this was the first time she'd been in a professional setting and hadn't felt judged and hadn't felt like crawling out the door afterward. At this time there was less laughter in her voice, so perhaps the laughter had much to do with a degree of apprehension that, in this interview, she would again be subject to negative judgment in the guise of expert knowledge.

Harlene: Let me ask you one more question. You said psychological explanations are roadblocks to rich story development. So are you talking about any kind of psychological explanations, or are you referring to psychological explanations in terms of pathological or negative ones?

Michael: I was referring to psychological explanations as a phenomenon of the 20th century, to those explanations that represent people's actions in life to be behaviors that are a surface manifestation of certain elements or essences that are considered to reside at the center of the "self," that are considered to constitute the core of the "self." It is interesting that this phenomenon of the 20th century was discontinuous with the psychology of 19th-century psychologists, and here I am particularly thinking of William James. James developed a psychology of inner experience that wasn't metaphysical in

that his account of the self was not founded on constructions of internal "dynamics" or on the idea of "core" and
relatively invariant self. I mention James here, because it is
often assumed that one cannot have psychological explanations of expressions of life that do not construct people's
actions as surface manifestations of elements or essences of a
psyche that are of the core of the self. And yet this is clearly
not the case.

When I speak of psychological explanations as roadblocks to rich story development, I am referring to these
20th-century developments in human understandings that
reference action to these elements and essences of the self.
These understandings are a roadblock to the social and relational history of what people are giving value to in their
acts of living, of what they hold precious, and of what they
intend for their lives.

Harlene: That's what I was thinking, but I wanted to check it out.

Michael: You want to say something, Jaakko?

Jaakko: Yes or no, but I choose not to say it. It was only a theoretical idea that started in my mind. I was so grateful that you
referred to William James, because his ideas are, in a way,
coming back.

Michael: Thank you. These reflections were all thought provoking.

International Outsider Thoughts

Yishai Shalif: What caught my attention most in Michael's presentation is the notion of practice. As part of the first reflection
Michael gives a short explanation on his take on Michel
Foucault. "He argues very much that constructions of
knowledge are always associated with practices . . . I think
that there are constructs of the world and I think there are
practices of living with those constructs. These practices of
living are like skills of living or self-formation that are associated with these constructs."

The notion of practice has always been close to my heart.
As someone practicing the Jewish code of law, I have found

this notion very close to Jewish religion that is much more practice than faith oriented. The new revelation for me in Michael's explanation is that practice is not only what the therapist does, but that it is a lens through which we view the way people actively form their lives and identities.

When Colin, at the beginning of the interview, says he has been behaving a lot better, from a practice lens, Michael asks, "What does behaving a lot better mean, like what?" He is focusing on how this practice of behaving a lot better is practiced. This way of looking at things opens up for me multiple starting points and understandings of the practices or initiatives that are all around one's life.

I'm writing this reflection in the midst of the beginning of a Jewish new year. This is a time when a Jew reflects on the previous year and decides what new directions and new changes he would like to make. In this process, the notion of specific small practices is central. One is not supposed to think of very big steps and changes since usually if it is not a specific and small practice, one has little chance to keep up to it. When writing this reflection I went through some pages of sessions I have had lately, and it is no wonder that I found myself time after time asking, "So how did you do it? What exactly does it look like? What specific steps does this entail? So what do you mean it is better?"

Even when referring to externalized problems, this notion of practices comes to help. So when a woman spoke about the fears that her husband will have a psychotic breakdown again, I asked, "How does fear convince you? What are its specific tactics (practices)?"

In conclusion, Michael has succeeded, through the written word, to scaffold my understanding and, through it, my practices of the notion of practice. It is not just what the therapist does, it is what we are all the time doing while forming and re-forming our lives.

John Gurnaes: The redefinition of human systems from cybernetic to linguistic and meaning-making systems marked the "linguistic turn" in a part of the field of family therapy and was a giant step. It was a step that brought language and meaning-making into focus in therapy. It was an almost "obvious" step in the sense that therapy is a meeting between two or more people in language. This step, together with Harry Goolishian's words, "Listen to what they really say, and not to what they really mean," brought therapy to "the surface." It was an important step away from the hermeneutics of suspiciousness that honored therapists who did not believe what clients said or did not believe in the validity of clients' own knowledges. Michael White brings all this a step further by his interest in the narrative. Again, this seems as an almost obvious step because what clients bring into therapy are stories about themselves, their relationships, and their lives.

What caught my attention in the first part of Michael's presentation was the thought "It's not my role to tell the family a new story about their life. That's not my job. It's not my job to point out positives or to congratulate people, or to focus on strength and resources. This is not my role." In this way Michael steps away from the immediate temptation to be the more or less primary author of good resourceful stories that he could offer the families in exchange for the bad ones. This practice does not offer people or families positive stories from out of nowhere. A reason for this, among others, is that he doesn't consider stories told by people to be constructs as they just as well could have been constructed in another way. Michael does not put himself in such a constructivist position. He says, "I think the constructivist position is that everything is constructed in language, and that we only have construction."

What catches my attention in his words is that "it's only a construction" is a very recognizable "trap" within a constructivist position in the field of family therapy when it comes to the understanding of language and knowledge. What I mean by this is that the critique of a representational or more or less naive-realistic understanding of language and knowledge is a central part of the general constructivist position. Our language and knowledge are not representations or pictures of something in the world but rather constructions. But if such a critique is not followed by an alternative theory of language and knowledge, a constructivist position on language and knowledge easily collapses into skepticism, antirealism, idealism, or relativism. Such a position is just the other side of the coin that doesn't add anything new to what it criticizes and because of that easily ends up in more or less implicit positions like "it's only a construction." This took me back to Wittgenstein's philosophy of language, which offers an alternative to a representational "picture-theory" of language without collapsing into skepticism, antirealism, idealism, or relativism.

Wittgenstein argued against the idea that the primary relation of language is to "the world." The concept "the world" is a construct within philosophy, which has put us in a position as outsiders to the world in which we live and which provided us with another dichotomy to solve. It became the primary job of language and knowledge to bridge this gap, and a lot of philosophy is about how we do this or about why it is not possible to do. What Wittgenstein did was to step out of this dichotomy by arguing that the primary relation of language was not to something called "the world" but to "practice." This did not mean that Wittgenstein argued against knowledge or science or against talking about true or false statements. He just meant that "the world" had nothing to do with our decisions about whether our statements are true or false statements. "The world" does not provide our statements with certainty. "The world" does not congratulate us for our findings. It's our project, our constructions, and our responsibility. The criteria for what counts as true or false statements are implicit decisions within our use of language, which always goes on within certain practices. Science is such a practice. Science goes on in language, and scientists agree on the language they use to make certain distinctions, as they agree on how to do the research and on the criteria for how to decide whether the one or the other statement is true. Other scientists agree on this or criticize it, and science goes on. So, in this way, science is a practice among other practices and the decisions made are made within these practices. Because of that, the questions that the sciences try to find answers to are practical questions such as "Does the world turn around the sun or the sun around the world?" "What is an atom?" and so on. These are all practical questions within the practice of science that scientists try to figure out. This has nothing to do with the metaphysical world–us dichotomy, but has a lot to do with scientific practice, theory, as well as with the politics of science, which is another story.

Because Wittgenstein, with his philosophy of language and knowledge, stepped out of the world–us dichotomy, his philosophy of language and knowledge did not move him into skepticism, relativism, or antirealism. This is important. Not to step out of the dichotomy has the implication within the logic set up by the dichotomy: that is, not to agree on some version of a representationalistic understanding of language and knowledge. This bridges the gap between "the world" and "us," turns people who do that into skepticists or antirealists. From such positions, it is by definition impossible to say or know anything about anything. Skepticism, relativism, or antirealism is just "the other side of the coin" that keeps these positions within the metaphysics of the world–us dichotomy that they try to escape by arguing against a representational theory of language and knowledge. To end in such a position is a serious "trap" for the use of a "constructivist" position within traditions of family therapy because it makes it difficult for these traditions to know something about what it is doing and why it easily makes it almost natural to see clients' expressions of their lives as "only constructions." Wittgenstein takes us to another place.

Because we can't use language without knowing anything, it is an implication of Wittgenstein's argument that the primary relation of language is to our "practice." Our use of language expresses the knowledges associated with these practices. This is the track Michael is on by pointing out that stories the family members tell express their knowledges and that such knowledges always are associated to practices. I think Michael's Foucault-inspired examples of this connection are a clear illustration of what this is about. Stories are "not just constructions" and it's not the job of a therapist to deny or change such knowledges or to try to replace them with a better or more positive knowledge from out of nowhere. "In my perspective it's not the therapist that is the constructor; rather the therapist provides the scaffolding for family members to become the constructors, the primary authors of the stories of their life and identity."

The traces Michael is referring to are thin traces from some of the 97% initiatives that are not taken up, acknowledged, or richly known in clients, often problem-saturated dominant stories. I really like this formulation, because it's a clear experience from daily life. A lot of our initiatives become stalled initiatives because they do not have a place, or can't be provided with meaning within our dominant stories about ourselves, our relationships, or life in general. Michael says people need to stand on a platform, and he considers it as his job as a therapist to contribute to the identification of and to the rich story development of such initiatives. This won't happen spontaneously. But because these knowledges are relevant to addressing the problems clients are addressing the therapist about, it's the therapist's job to provide a scaffold for the development of such stories. "It's in the rich story development that people have a familiarity with these knowledges of their history." It's the job of a therapist to assist clients to move from the known to what is possible to know. It's not the job of a therapist to give advice, make interventions, or be respectful, give acknowledgment, be empathetic, or join other popular norms for therapists' attitudes that makes it ideal for therapists to act and sound like they are "the re-appearance of Christ." What usually is called "respect," "acknowledgement," and "empathy" grows naturally out of the way Michael in his therapeutic practice stays within clients' knowledges and practices as well as out of his understanding of human beings as being multiknowledged. It's not the job for the therapist to deny or to try to change certain "not-very-nice" knowledges about life that clients can have for the purpose of providing clients with more positive or resourceful stories about themselves from out of nowhere. To do that is to keep the client within the dominant story and is not to assist clients in identifying and developing rich stories about initiatives and knowledges that didn't have a place and a meaning within the dominant story.

This focus on "scaffolding" comes from Michael's interest in Vygotsky's zone of proximal development, which he considers to be a relevant concept for the therapeutic practice. I think he demonstrates such relevance in a clear way in his conversation with Martha and Colin. I think that these ideas are highly relevant for any learning. In my opinion Michael is expanding Vygotsky's concept into what he calls "the zone of proximal story development" by seeing the same implications of rich story development as Vygotsky saw in the developments of concepts. Concepts, or stories, make a kind of platform from where it is possible for a person to distance himself or herself from the known and familiar in a way that makes it possible to intervene in and shape his or her own life. I think that this is what is of importance to Michael in therapy: to assist clients in living a life that they prefer. To me an important type of questioning that scaffolds such a therapeutic intention is Michael's evaluating questioning like, "Is this development a good development for your life and your future?" or "Is this ok for you?" This type of questioning that runs through the conversation with Martha and Colin assists them in positioning themselves in relation to their own life in a way that makes it possible for them to intervene in their life and give shape to it.

According to Michael, the gap between the known and what is possible to know cannot be traversed outside of the context of social collaboration. He says that one of the partners in that social collaboration is required to have the skills relevant to the scaffolding of this gap. In families it's the adults that have this role in relation to their children, and this is exactly the role Michael gives back to Martha in his conversation with Martha and Colin. He does this by asking Martha, "What sort of development would you say this is? How would you name this sort of development? You see your son being able to take time out but at the same time stay active, not shut down, and have an effect of his future. What name ... ?" To Martha the name was "self-control." In the conversation, the same happened with Martha's introduction of the concept of "personal freedom." By doing this, Michael takes the idea of the zone of proximal development and brings it into conversations with families in a very direct way. By doing this he steps away from being the primary or only "scaffold-builder" in his conversation with the family.

Note: Michael White passed away suddenly before he was able to craft a response to the international outsider comments.

5

CLOSING TRIALOGUE

Scot: The exchange in Finland documented in this book marked an intersection in time among our collaborationists. As such, they were able to take a moment and reflect upon each other's practices and teaching. As audience members and discussants, they were provided with what Michael would call a "reflexive distance" in a sense, an opportunity to step back from their own teaching outside of the immediacy of its demands to achieve a different vantage point. I imagine this could have offered them a range of considerations about their own work and their colleagues' work.

In my mind, the frontier these three have developed continues to offer an alternative to modernistic approaches steeped in normalizing judgment, pathologizing, and singular descriptions of life and experience. In many ways, their work is the counterstory to more colonizing schools of therapeutic practice that outline strict guides with regard to how to "do the work." I am not suggesting guidance is not important but rather a supporting part to the development of the craft. I've always thought facilitating therapeutic conversations is more art than science. I recognize my bias for this; however, within these chapters the structure that supports the art came clearer for me.

I'd like to hear from you both, as you reflect back on these chapters and the points of convergence, divergence, and overlap: What stands out for you? What do these ideas and exchanges suggest about what is possible in therapeutic practice?

Tapio: Could it be that the "reflexive distance" created through this stepping back from the immediacy of our experiences offers

171

us a very interesting and freeing position as a spectator in a movie titled *The Melodrama of My Life*? From this vantage point into our ordinary, ego-centered presence, we can see and experience series of pictures that appear and disappear on a screen called our mind in the light of the consciousness. By identifying with these ideas, beliefs, convictions, opinions, feelings, and so on, we create a virtual world and experience that to be our reality. Instead of sense-related "realities," what we perceive is in fact a mental construction of our own mind. The self in this virtual reality we often begin to accept as a single, separate substance or entity having essential, unchanging properties. Could we say that the "reflective distance" and the deconstructive practices along with it can help us to avoid being captured by the taken-for-granted, by culturally and historically conditioned thoughts and concepts, descriptions of life, and instead be with what is as it is? From this position there is an opportunity to see and to experience the self and the world as consisting solely of processes. A process is not a thing, entity, or being but rather an event, activity, or becoming, a special movement within the world, interconnected with other movements and in constant change in every respect. From this position we are also able to ask, without power struggles, questions like the following: What are the most common normalizing judgments or things that we take for granted and never question in our practice but which constantly affect the way we look and what we see? What does our "internalized gaze" look like? How do we police ourselves as therapists?

Michael White was once asked what *goals* mean to him in psychotherapy. This is what he answered:

> If I planned to go to a conference, and if I knew beforehand what I would be thinking at the end, then I wouldn't go. It is like that with my work. If I knew where we would be at the end of the session, I don't think I would do this work. And if I had not changed at all after the session, then my actions

probably would not have a very big impact on the people who came to me. (White, 2000, p. 138)

Similarly, the American poet and psychotherapist Dvorah Simon described her work in the mid-1990s:

> Therapy is a spiritual path on which we suddenly realize that we are something full-bodied, as it were something with guts, something that makes you suddenly realize that you are breathing... that your awareness encompasses time and as it is embraced with it, that something is beautiful or absurd or magnificent, or ridiculous, and every inch of you is moving through space, and knows, and doesn't know that it knows... (Simon, 1995, p. 2).

And for this we get paid as therapists!

Many years ago my supervisor asked me a question that was to become one of the turning points in my career as a therapist. "Tapio, what did your client do that helped you to work as a therapist the way you did?" After this I started to ask myself questions like: What has my wife done that I have become this kind of husband? What have the pupils done in the classroom that has created this kind of a teacher? Could it be that the therapist is creating himself or herself creating the client, and the client creates himself or herself creating the therapist? So the zone of proximal development is not dual, but mutual or non-dual space. In this zone the therapist and the client arise to meet each other in each and every moment. They arise in the ways of collaborating with each other. In these existential meetings, the selves of people are empty, emerging in response to immediate experience, and this direct, non-dual experience gives us an opportunity to deeply realize our selves in the others. If we as therapists concentrate more on how to be in our work compared with how to do it, I think—and sometimes I have also experienced, like Dvorah has—that our work becomes an exercise of ethics, an art where instead of control and fear, insecurity and not-knowing can be transformed into a wonder and wisdom of life itself.

Frank: Tapio, this reminds me of common historical ground *all* of us share, including Tom, Harlene, and Michael: systemic connection. Your beautiful description of the mutual influence between teacher and student took me back decades. I do see second-order cybernetics as a useful metaphor when describing the work of these three ingenious and compassionate theorists because they continually changed in response to dialogues with clients, interactions with colleagues, and innovation influenced by new philosophies. How could one *not* be changed when witnessing the experiences of Bosnian women? Or oppressed First Peoples? Or abused children? To remain the same would assume (a) we are not influenced, and (b) there is a unified, static self. What these masterful people—and you, my colleagues—have done is push me once again to re-view. I am re-viewing my sense of self-in-the-world, my place in this history-building project, and my relationship to these provocative ideas. I have been influenced by these pioneers, and my sense of self has been shifted toward greater engagement, thoughtful responses, and careful listening.

You made another marvelous statement, that "our work becomes an exercise of ethics." This also takes me back to one of the giants in our common past, to the late physicist Heinz von Foerster. He gave us what he called the ethical imperative: "Act always so as to increase the number of choices" (von Foerster, 1984, p. 308). I see this happening throughout this book: principals, outsider commentators, and editors constantly seeking to create more choices in understanding and action. This book reminds me of the constancy of change and our charge to artfully and ethically contribute to this inevitability. My learning should return to others, and the wisdom I receive from students, colleagues, and (especially) clients should recur in my writing, social encounters, and close relationships.

And Scot, your question is intriguing: "What do these ideas and exchanges suggest about what is possible in therapeutic practice?" Studying the case examples, listening to the stories, and reading the transcripts bring me *hope*... and hope is a vital ingredient in therapeutic practice that I am continuing to nurture. Meta-research studies consistently show that the major sources of change in therapeutic practice are the client's own resources and the therapist–client relationship. What I bring as the clinician are ways to intervene and hope, the other two major contributors to change. I have come to see through this book that I need to focus on being hope-full. I know how to form relationships; I already draw from clients' resources, strengths, and resiliencies; and my studies on ways to intervene in psychotherapy have probably overdeveloped a dependency on doing. Hope, for me, is being. As Tapio and I have written elsewhere (Malinen & Thomas, 2009), being encompasses doing, like ethics must frame our actions. I *am* hope-full—for a more compassionate therapeutic community, for more witnessing and less pragmatism, for more choice and less control, and for more dialogue and fewer speeches.

Honestly, I have no idea what is possible—the possible is beyond my imagination. I simply know that the possible is not limited by what *is* or by what *was*. When I began in this field, I could not imagine the directions we are taking now or the positive and far-reaching impact of pioneers like Michael, Tom, and Harlene. So, my wisdom: Dream it. Play. Witness. Never be content. Listen. Increase options. Bring compassion. And be open. Then, magic happens.

Scot: Frank, your invitation to dream, play, witness, and never be content seems like a fitting place to end our short discussion. With the passing of two of our primary contributors, we are left with two tremendous treasure chests of work to sift through and carry forward. However, I don't imagine any of our protagonists would support static representations and replications of their work. They would want others to continue crafting their craft. Perhaps Michael's seemingly unquenchable thirst for ideas will inspire others to push the boundaries of their fields of knowledge to reclaim their curiosity and their sense of great adventure in crafting their therapeutic conversational art. Perhaps Tom's passion for the undiscovered universe within a word can call practitioners to reach toward the possibilities in meaning making in conversations. Harlene's teachings continue to inspire, reaching across borders and seeking out dialogue as a way to generate possibility and explore knowledge.

To me, great ideas emerge from the coming together of one's thoughts with others' ideas across disciplines and through time. Our principal contributors have brought their ideas forward, ideas that had likely percolated and stewed for long periods. These ideas were infused by what they took from their influences and experiences. They were not likely grand strokes of genius but rather what emerged from considerable contemplation, exhausting hard work/rework, and extensive practice of their art. Perhaps this is the greater calling that collectively they offer to the practitioner, experienced or new to the field: Put in the time to hone your craft, not settling for certainties. Push the ideas through experimentation, practice, and by networking with your own collective. Have dialogue about the ideas and practices, as it's through dialogue that something known can morph to something possible to know. And lastly, pay attention to the ethic of the practice. How do we craft our presence and practice in a way that is most respectful, hope-friendly, and acknowledging the identity project we engage in during any therapeutic conversation? These are important lessons most often taught through asking questions—intentional, well-crafted, and timely questions.

Tapio: For me, ending something is always a beginning of something else. To end with this beginning, I would like to leave readers and ourselves some questions for consideration.

How is my practice modifying the quality of my experience and deepening my understanding? Are my questions supporting dominant social practices, or are they creating alternatives? If we cannot stand outside of discourse, how can we be selective about which discourses fit better with our values and have less harmful effects on the wider community? Does my work as a therapist separate or unite people? What is the nature of "self" or "me" of the therapist, and the place of compassion in being with fellow human beings? Which is more important: what my colleagues think of me or how my clients experience me? How can I possibly listen to and understand another person if I am preoccupied with speaking? Could silence or quieting my mind take away my (illusory) sense of security and control and open me to the untidiness, contradictions, and richness of being that cannot be bound by conceptual ordering? Could silence invite me to the openness of "not knowing" and transform me in order to know rather than objectify the world in order to recognize me in my cognitive conceptual immobility?

References

Amundson, J., Stewart, K., & Valentine, L. (1993). Temptations of power and certainty. *Journal of Marital and Family Therapy, 19*(2), 111–123.

Andersen, T. (1995). Acts of forming and informing. In S. Friedman (Ed.), *The reflecting team in action* (pp. 11–37). New York: Guilford Press.

Andersen, T. (1997). Researching client-therapist relationships: A collaborative study for informing therapy. *Journal of Systemic Therapies, 16*(2), 125–133.

Andersen, T. (2007a). Crossroads: Tom Andersen in conversation with Per Jensen. In H. Anderson & P. Jensen (Eds.), *Innovations in the reflecting process* (pp. 158–174). London: Karnac.

Andersen, T. (2007b). Human participating: Human "being" is the step for human "becoming" in the next step. In H. Anderson & D. Gehart (Eds.), *Collaborative therapy: Relationships and conversations that make a difference* (pp. 81–93). New York: Routledge.

Anderson, H. (1997). *Conversation, language, and possibilities: A postmodern approach to therapy.* New York: Basic Books.

Anderson, H. (2001). *Becoming a postmodern collaborative therapist: A clinical and theoretical journey, Part II.* Retrieved March 1, 2011, from http://www.harleneanderson.org/writings/becomingpartii.htm

Anderson, H. (2005). The myth of not-knowing. *Family Process, 44,* 497–504.

Anderson, H. (2007a). The heart and spirit of collaborative therapy: The philosophical stance—"A way of being" in relationship and conversation. In H. Anderson & D. Gehart (Eds.), *Collaborative therapy: Relationships and conversations that make a difference* (pp. 43–59). New York: Routledge.

Anderson, H. (2007b). Tom David Andersen: Fragments of his influence and inspiration. *Journal of Marital and Family Therapy, 33,* 411–416.

Anderson, H., & Gehart, D. R. (Eds.). (2006). *Collaborative therapy: Relationships and conversations that make a difference.* New York: Routledge.

Anderson, H., & Goolishian, H. (1988). Human systems as linguistic systems: Evolving ideas about the implications for theory and practice. *Family Process, 27,* 371–393.

Anderson, H., & Goolishian, H. (1988). Human systems as linguistic systems: Preliminary and evolving ideas about the implications for clinical theory. *Family Process, 27,* 371–393.

Anderson, H., & Goolishian, H. (Ed.). (1992). *Från påverkan till medverkan* [From the impact of participation]. Stockholm: Mareld.

Bakhtin, M. (1981). *The dialogic imagination.* Austin: University of Texas Press.

Foucault, M. (1979). *Discipline and punish: The birth of the prison.* Middlesex, UK: Peregrine Books.

Foucault, M. (1980). *Power/knowledge: Selected interviews and other writings.* New York: Pantheon Books.

Foucault, M. (1984). *The history of sexuality.* Great Britain: Peregrine Books.

Foucault, M. (1986). *The history of sexuality.* London: Peregrine Books.

Harkaway, J. E. (1987). *Eating disorders.* Rockville, MD: Aspen.

Hoffman, L. (2002). *Family therapy: An intimate history.* New York: Norton.

Keeney, B. P., Thomas, F. N., Strano, J., Ridenour, N., Morris, J., McKenzie, P., et al. (1987). A cybernetic approach to weight control. In J. E. Harkaway (Ed.), *Eating disorders* (pp. 84–92). Rockville, MD: Aspen.

Kolstad, A. (Ed.). (1995). *I sporet av det uendelige. En debattbok om Emmanuel Levinas.* [In the track of the infinite.]. Oslo, Norway: H. Aschehougs forlag.

Lysack, M. (2008). Relational mindfulness and dialogical space in family therapy. In S. F. Hick & T. Bien (Eds.), *Mindfulness and the therapeutic relationship* (pp. 141–158). New York: Guilford Press.

Mahrer, A. R. (1987). These are the components of any theory of psychotherapy. *Journal of Integrative and Eclectic Psychotherapy, 6*(1), 28–31.

Malinen, T. (2004). The Wisdom of Not Knowing—A Conversation with Harlene Anderson. *Journal of Systemic Therapies,* Vol. 23, No. 2, New York: The Guilford Press.

Malinen, T., & Thomas, F. N. (2009). Doing therapy: A source of therapist well-being. *CONTEXT, 47,* 24–29.

Maturana, H. R., & Poerksen, B. (2004). The view of the systemicist: A conversation. *Journal of Constructivist Psychology, 17,* 269–279.

McNamee, S. (2004). Social construction as practical theory: Lessons for practice and reflection in psychotherapy. In D. Paré & G. Larne (Eds.), *Collaborative practice in psychology and therapy* (pp. 9–21). London: Haworth Clinical Practice Press.

Myerhoff, B. (1982). Life history among the elderly: Performance, visibility, and re-membering. In J. Ruby (Ed.), *A crack in the mirror: Reflective perspectives in anthropology* (pp. 99–117). Philadelphia: University of Pennsylvania Press.

Myerhoff, B. (1986). Life not death in Venice: Its second life. In V. Turner & E. Bruner (Eds.) *The anthropology of experience* (pp. 261–286). Chicago: University of Illinois Press.

Nhat Hanh, T. (1987). *Being peace.* Berkeley, CA: Parallax Press.

Øvreberg, G., & Andersen, T. (Ed.). (1986). *Aadel Bülow-Hansen's fysioterapi.* [Aadel Bülow-Hansen's physiotherapy]. Tromsø, Oslo: I kommisjon med Norli forlag.

Paré, D. (2010). *Just talk: Developing skills in culturally mindful helping.* Unpublished manuscript.

Paré, D., Richardson, B., & Tarragona, M. (2009). Watching the train: Mindfulness and inner dialogue in therapist skills training. In S. F. Hick (Ed.), *Mindfulness and social work* (pp. 76–91). Chicago: Lyceum Books.

Penn, P. (1994). Creating a participant text: Writing, multiple voices, narrative multiplicity. *Family Process, 33*(3), 217–232.

Penn, P. (2001). Chronic illness: Trauma, language and writing: Breaking the silence. *Family Process, 40*(1), 33–52.

Rosenbaum, R., & Dyckman, J. (1996). No self! No problem! Actualizing empty self in psychotherapy. In M. Hoyt (Ed.), *Constructive therapies* (Vol. 2, pp. 238–274). New York: Guilford Press.

Seikkula, J. (1995). Treating psychosis by means of open dialogue. In S. Friedman (Ed.), *The reflecting team in action* (pp. 62–80). New York: Guilford Press.

Seikkula, J., Alakare, B., & Aaltonen, J. (2001a). El enfoque del diálogo abierto. Principios y resultados de investigación sobre un primer episidio psicótico [Foundations of open dialogue: Main principles and research results with first episode psychosis]. *Sistemas Familiares, 17,* 75–87.

Seikkula, J., Alakare, B., & Aaltonen, J. (2001b). Open dialogue in psychosis I: An introduction and case illustration. *Journal of Constructivist Psychology, 14,* 247–266.

Seikkula, J., Alakare, B., & Aaltonen, J. (2001c). Open dialogue in psychosis II: A comparison of good and poor outcome. *Journal of Constructivist Psychology, 14,* 267–284.

Seikkula, J., Alakare, B., & Haarakangas, K. (2001). When clients are diagnosed "schizophrenetic." In B. Duncan & J. Sparks (Eds.), *Heroic clients, heroic agencies: Partnership for change.* Ft. Lauderdale, FL: Nova Southeastern University Press.

Shotter, J. (2007). *Not to forget Tom Andersen's way of being Tom Andersen: The importance of what "just happens" to us.* Paper presented at The 12th International Meeting on the Treatment of Psychosis, August 29, Palanga, Lithuania.

Simon, D. (1995). Doing therapy as spiritual path. *News of the Difference, 4*(1), 1–5.

von Foerster, H. (1984). On constructing a reality. In *Observing Systems* (pp. 287–309). Seaside, CA: Intersystems Publications.

Vygotsky, L. (1986). *Thought and language.* Cambridge: MIT Press.

White, M. (1985). Fear busting and monster taming: An approach to the fears of young children. *Dulwich Centre Review,* 29–34. Republished in White, M. (1989). *Selected papers* (pp. 107–113). Adelaide, Australia: Dulwich Centre Publications.

White, M. (1987). Anorexia nervosa: A cybernetic perspective. In J. E. Harkaway (Ed.), *Eating disorders* (pp. 117–129). Rockville, MD: Aspen.

White, M. (1989). Pseudo-encopresis: From avalanche to victory, from vicious to virtuous cycles. In *Selected Papers* (pp. 115–124). Adelaide, Australia: Dulwich Centre Publications. Original work published in 1984, *Family Systems Medicine, 2*(2).

White, M. (2000). *Reflections of narrative practice: Essays and interviews.* Adelaide, Australia: Dulwich Centre Publications.

White, M. (2004a). Folk psychology and narrative practice. In *Narrative practice and exotic lives: Resurrecting diversity in everyday life* (pp. 59–118). Adelaide, Australia: Dulwich Centre Publications.

White, M. (2004b). Narrative practice, couple therapy and conflict dissolution. In M. White, *Narrative practice and exotic lives: Resurrecting diversity in everyday life* (pp. 1–41). Adelaide, Australia: Dulwich Centre Publications.

White, M. (2007). *Maps of narrative practice.* New York: Norton.

White, M., & Epston, D. (1990). *Narrative means to therapeutic ends.* New York: Norton.

White, M., & Epston, D. (1992). Introduction. In *Experience, contradiction, narrative & imagination: Selected papers of David Epston and Michael White* (pp. 7–9). Adelaide, Australia: Dulwich Centre Publications.

White, M., & Morgan, A. (2006). *Narrative therapy with children and their families.* Adelaide, Australia: Dulwich Centre Publications.

Wittgenstein, L. (1953). *Philosophical investigations.* Oxford, UK: Blackwell.

Wittgenstein, L. (1968). *Philosophical investigations* (3rd ed.). New York: Macmillan.

Index

CPSIA information can be obtained
at www.ICGtesting.com
Printed in the USA
FSOW02n0620301116
27923FS